Ordinary Life in Mughal India

The Evidence from Painting

Ordinary Life in Mughal India

The Evidence from Painting

S.P. Verma

ARYAN BOOKS INTERNATIONAL
New Delhi

ORDINARY LIFE IN MUGHAL INDIA

ISBN: 978-81-7305-424-2

Published in **2012** by:

ARYAN BOOKS INTERNATIONAL
Pooja Apartments, 4B, Ansari Road, New Delhi - 110 002 (India)
Tel.: 23287589, 23255799; Fax: 91-11-23270385
E-mail: aryanbooks@gamil.com
www.aryanbooks.co.in

Printed in India at Mudrak, Delhi-110091

Remembering

Kunwar Muhammad Ashraf

"It is now coming to be universally recognized that nothing is 'beneath the dignity' of history's notice or outside the scope of its ken, and that all the doings and suffering of mankind in every walk of the life are proper subjects for a historian to investigate."

Kunwar Muhammad Ashraf, *Life and Conditions of the People of Hindustan,* New Delhi, Reprint, 1970, p. 6.

Preface

An inspiration for the present endeavour gathered from K.M. Ashraf's approach to history, that is, "It is now coming to be universally recognized that nothing is 'beneath the dignity' of history's notice or outside the scope of its ken, and that all the doings and suffering of mankind in every walk of the life are proper subjects for a historian to investigate", drived me in the times of sixteenth and seventeenth centuries to correspond with his work (*Life and Condition of the People of Hindustan*, Delhi, 1959). Further, I being equipped with the research experience involved in the production of the volume *Art and Material Culture in the Paintings of Akbar's Court* (New Delhi, 1978), and the preparation of an exhibition, *Everyday Life and Work* (Aligarh, 1985) followed by a souvenir *India at Work* for the delegates of Indian History Congress (55th Session, Aligarh, 1994) prompted me ahead to construct a history of country-men and - women largely based on the evidence of contemporary paintings.

For an understanding of painting as a source of history, I owe much to my teachers Emeritus Professor S. Nurul Hasan (Late) and Emeritus Professor Irfan Habib.

I thankfully acknowledge the support of the Indian Council of Historical Research, New Delhi, for extending to me with the award of the Senior Fellowship for two years (2005 and 2006) to accomplish the present study.

Special thanks are due to Professor Shahbuddin Iraqi, Centre of Advanced Study, Department of History, Aligarh Muslim University for kindly providing me all facilities at the Seminar Library of the Department.

I am equally indebted to Mr. Shakeel Ahmad Khan, Librarian, Maulana Azad Library (A.M.U.) who facilitated me with an access to the rare collections of books and Indian miniatures lodged at the Library.

Special thanks are due to Professor Shireen Moosvi, Professor Pushpa Prasad and Dr. Ishrat Alam for their sincere and friendly support and keen interest in my work.

A note of thanks is due to Mr. Arshad Ali, Muniruddin Khan, Ghulam Mujtaba and Idris Beg who ungrudgely helped me and took care of my study material.

I record my sincere gratitude to my family and especially to Dr. Smriti Prasad and her daughters, Astha and Ami, who always cared for me despite my disregard to them.

Finally, I am thankful to Mr. Vikas Arya, Aryan Books International, New Delhi for his understanding and making the present work accessible to a wider readership.

Som Prakash Verma
Emeritus Fellow in History
Aligarh Muslim University

Aligarh

Contents

List of Abbreviations

AA	*Artibus Asiae,* Hellerau-Dresden, subsequently Ascona
AAA	*Archives of Asian Art,* London
AAL	*Art and Letters,* Journal of the Royal India, Pakistan and Ceylon Society, London
AAS	*Arts Asiatiques,* Musee Guimet, Paris
AEI	*Athar-e Iran,* Haarlem
AIS	*Ars Islamica,* Ann Arbor, U.S.A.
AOA	*Arts of Asia,* Arts of Asia Publications, Hong Kong
AOS	*Ars Orientalis,* Freer Gallery of Art, Washington, D.C.
Apollo	*Apollo,* London
AQ	*Art Quarterly,* Institute of Arts, Detroit, U.S.A.
ASA	*Arts Asiatiques,* Ascona
BAAC	Birla Academy of Art and Culture, Calcutta
BBSM	*Bulletin of the Baroda State Museum,* Baroda
BCA	*Bulletin of the College of Arts,* Baghdad
BCMA	*Bulletin of the Cleveland Museum of Art,* Cleveland
BDCRI	*Bulletin of the Deccan College Research Institute,* Poona
BFAM	*Bulletin of the Fogg Art Museum,* Cambridge, Mass
BIM	*Indian Museum Bulletin,* Calcutta
BKB	Bharat Kala Bhavan, Banaras Hindu University, Varanasi
BLACM	*Bulletin of the Los Angeles Country Museum of Art,* New York
BLO	Bodleian Library, Oxford
BM	British Museum and Library, London
BMB	Brooklyn Museum, Brooklyn, New York
BMFA	*Bulletin of the Museum of Fine Arts,* Boston
BMMA	*Bulletin of the Metropolitan Museum of Art,* New York
BMQ	*British Museum Quarterly,* London
BNP	Bibliotheque Nationale, Paris
BPWM	*Bulletin of the Prince of Wales Museum of Western India,* Mumbai
BSOAS	*Bulletin of the School of Oriental and African Studies,* London
BUM	*Burlington Magazine,* London
BVM	*Bulletin of the Victoria Memorial Hall,* Calcutta

CANH	Alice and Nasli Heeramaneck Collection, New York
CBL	Chester Beatty Library, Dublin
CBLA	Album of Separate Miniatures of the Mughal School, Chester Beatty Library, Dublin
CHJ	*Calcutta Historical Journal*, Calcutta
EAQ	*Eastern Art Quarterly*, Philadelphia
EW	*East and West*, Rome
EWA	*Encyclopaedia of World Art*
GM	*Geographical Magazine*, London
Hamza	*Hamzanama*; or *Dastan-i Amir Hamza*
IAL	*Indian Arts and Letters* (1927-1947), London, subsequently *Arts and Letters: India and Pakistan*, Royal India Society Journal
IHR	*The Indian Historical Review*, New Delhi
INI	*Indo-Iranica*, Journal of the Iran Society, Calcutta
IPM (A)	Album of Indian and Persian Miniatures of the 16th-18th Centuries
ISC	*Islamic Culture*, Hyderabad
JAOS	*Journal of the American Oriental Society*
JBNHS	*Journal of the Bombay Natural History Society*, Madras
JBORS	*Journal of the Bihar and Orissa Research Society*, Patna
JIA	*Journal of Indian Art*, London
JIAI	*Journal of Indian Art and Industry*, London
JIM	*Journal of Indian Museum*, Calcutta
JISOA	*Journal of Indian Society and Oriental Art*, Calcutta
JNES	*Journal of Near Eastern Studies*, Chicago
JPH	*Journal of the Pakistan Historical Society*, Karachi
JPHS	*Journal of the Punjab Historical Society*, Calcutta, subsequently Lahore
JRAS	*Journal of the Royal Asiatic Society*, London
JUB	*Journal of the University of Bombay*, Mumbai (formerly Bombay)
JUPHS	*Journal of the U.P. Historical Society*, London
JWAG	*Journal of the Walters Art Gallery*, Baltimore
LALIT	*Lalit-Kala*, New Delhi
MARG	*Marg*, Mumbai (formerly Bombay)
MMS	*Metropolitan Museum Studies*, New York
OA	*Oriental Art*, London
OAV	*Orientalistisches Archiv*, Leipzig
Orientations	*Orientations*, Hong Kong
Phoenix	*Phoenix*, Amsterdam
PIHC	*Proceedings of the Indian History Congress*
PQ	*Pakistan Quarterly*, Karachi
QRHS	*Quarterly Review of Historical Studies*, Calcutta
RAA	*Revue des Arts Asiatiques*, Paris
RLR	Raza Library, Rampur
ROOPA	*Roopa-Lekha*, New Delhi
RUPAM	*Rupam*, Calcutta
SAS	*South Asian Studies*, London
STUDIO	*Studio*, London
TIA	*Times of India Annual*, Bombay

List of Illustrations

COLOUR PLATES

Photo from Geeti Sen, *Paintings from the Akbarnama: A Visual Chronicle of Mughal India*, New Delhi, 1984, pl. 31.

VIII. Fathpur Sikri complex being built. *Akbarnama* (Mughal, *ca.* AD 1600-05), Victoria and Albert Museum, no.I.S. 2-1896, 86/117.
Note: masons, laboures, stone-cutters and women pounding the bricks and sieving the lime.
Photo from Geeti Sen, *Paintings from the Akbarnama: A Visual Chronicle of Mughal India*, New Delhi, 1984, pl. 61.

IX. The arrival of Nanda and his family (Mughal, *ca.* AD 1585-90). A folio from the *Harivamsha*. Lower part of the miniature. Virginia Museum of Fine Arts, The Nasli and Heeramanek Collection, Gift of Paul Mellon, 68.8.50.
Note: the women cooking, churning, and fondling with child.
Photo from Joseph M. Dye III, *The Arts of India, Virginia Museum of Fine Arts*, New Delhi, 2001, pp. 222-25, Cat no.74.

X. Milking of cows. Folio from a palm-leaf manuscript *Bhagavata Purana* (Orissa, *ca.* 17th century AD). British Museum, London, Or. 11689, f.1r.
Photo from D. Barrett and B. Gray, *Painting of India*, Cleveland, 1963, illustration, p. 74.

XI. Details from the miniature "Lord Krishna lifts mount Govardhan" (Mughal, *ca.* AD 1585-90). The Metropolitan Museum of Art, New York.
Note: women with spinning wheel, and the bullocks employed to carry the luggage.
Photo from S.C. Welch, *Imperial Mughal Painting*, New York, 1978, pl. 10.

XII. Details from a miniature "*Rubab* player, his companion, and a peasant" (Mughal, *ca.* AD 1620) by Bichitr. Victoria and Albert Museum, London, I.M. 27-1925.
Note: spinning wheel hung in the thatched roof of the mud house.
Photo from I. Stchoukine, *La Peinture Indienne 'a l' Epoque des Grands Moghols*, Paris, 1929, pl. 44.

XIII. From Gokul to Vrindaban (Kangra school, *ca.* AD 1750). National Museum, New Delhi.
Note: women carrying spinning wheel and worm-press.
Photo from M.S. Randhawa, *Kangra Paintings of the Bhagavata Purana*, Delhi, 1960, pl. V.

XIV. King Dara meeting herdsmen in a landscape (Mughal school, *ca.* AD 1610), H. Kevorkian Collection (lower part of miniature depicting plough-men and a woman at work).
Photo from Toby Falk, Simon Digby and Michael Goedhuis, *Paintings from Mughal India*, Colnaghi, London, no date, cat. no.18, p. 40.

XV. Bazaar astrologer with his clients (Mughal school, *ca.* 1590-95 AD). *Akhlaq-i Nasiri*, Prince Sadruddin Aga Khan Collection, Museum Rietberg Zurich.
Photo from B.N. Goswami and E. Fisher, *Wunder ainer Goldenen Zeit, Malaerei am Hof der Moghul Kaiser, Indische Kunst des 16, und 17. Jahrhunderts aus Schweizer Sammlungen*, Zurich, 1987, pl. 58.

XVI. Rejoicing on the birth of Prince Salim at Fathpur Sikri (detail from the lower part of the miniature). (Mughal school, *ca.* AD 1600-05), Victoria and Albert Museum, London, no.IS 2-1896, 78/117.
Note: the crowd of men, women and children rushing to collect alms. See also the disabled beggar supporting himself on hand-shoes.
Photo from Geeti Sen, *Paintings from the Akbarnama, A Visual Chronicle of Mughal India*, New Delhi, 1984, pl. 46.

XVII. Babur surveys the mausoleum in the environs of Delhi (Mughal, *ca.* AD 1598-1600). *Baburnama*, British Museum, London, Or. 3714, f. 370b.
Photo from Hamid Suleiman, *Miniature of Babur-nama*, Tashkent, 1970, pl. 54.

BLACK AND WHITE PLATES

Published: Karl Khandalavala and Moti Chandra, *New Documents of Indian Painting: A Reappraisal*, Bombay, 1969, fig. 179.

13. A farm scene. Folio from the *Mahapurana* (AD 1540). Sri Digambara Jain Atisaya Kshetra, Jaipur.
    Note: the cultivator driving the bullocks.
    Photo from Karl J. Khandalavala and Moti Chandra, *New Documents of Indian Painting: A Reappraisal*, Bombay, 1969, fig. 153.
14. A detail from a miniature "A camel rider rescuing the snake from fire", *Anwar-i Suhaili*, (Mughal, AD 1597). Bharat Kala Bhavan, Varanasi, No. 9069, f. 113.
    Photo from Rai Krishnadasa, *Anwar-e-Suhaili (Iyar-i-Danish)*, Varanasi, 1999, pl.H.
15. A detail from the miniature "A gigantic bird with a man in its claws", *Khamsa* of Nizami (Mughal, *ca.* AD 1595). British Museum, London, Or. 12208.
    Photo from J.M. Rogers, *Mughal Miniatures*, London, 1993, fig. 25.
16. Peasants harvesting crop (with sickle, threshing and winnowing). Detail from *Razmnama* (Mughal, *ca.* AD 1600). Chattrapati Shivaji Maharaj Vastu Sangrahalaya (formerly, Prince of Wales Museum), Mumbai, No. 43.35.
    Photo from Moti Chandra, *Indian Art*, Bombay, 1974, pl. XXXIII.
17. Building construction (Mughal, *ca.* AD 1600-05). Provenance unknown. Victoria and Albert Museum, London, no.IS 95-1965.
    Note: masons, labourers, water-carriers, carpenters and woman labourer.
    Photo from A.J. Qaisar, *Building Construction in Mughal India: The Evidence from Painting*, New Delhi, 1988, pl. 7.
18. Building construction (Mughal, *ca.* AD 1600-05). A detail from the folio of *Akbarnama*, Chester Beatty Library, Dublin.
    Photo from T.W. Arnold and J.V.S. Wilkinson, *Library of Chester Beatty: A Catalogue of the Indian Miniatures*, Vol. II, London, 1936, pl. 24.
19. Building construction (Mughal, *ca.* AD 1600-05). *Shahnama*, British Museum, Add. 5600, f.372a.
    Note: manson, iron-smiths and labourers at work.
    Photo from L. Binyon and T.W. Arnold, *The Court Painters of the Grand Moguls*, London, 1921, pls. pl. VIII.
20. Building construction. *Jami-ut Tawarikh* (Mughal, AD 1598), Gulistan Palace Library, Teheran.
    Note: masons, carpenters, water-carriers, labourers and women labourers at work.
    Photo from J. Marek *et al.*, *The Chenghis Khan Miniatures from the Court of Akbar the Great*, London, 1963, pl. 29.
21. Masons building a wall (Mughal, *ca.* AD 1600). Indian Museum, Kolkata (No. 201).
    Photo from Percy Brown, *Indian Painting under the Mughals, AD 1550 to AD 1750*, Oxford, 1924, pl. LIX, fig. 1.
22. A woman either kneading bread or grinding grain (after Vats, 1941). A figurine excavated from Harappa (*ca.* 2500-2000 BC).
    Photo from G.L. Possehl, *The Indus Civilization: A Contemporary Perspective*, New Delhi, 2002, p.182, fig. 10.10.
23. Mother holding a child (after Mackay, 1937-38). A figurine excavated from Mohenjo-daro (*ca.* 2500-2000 BC).
    Photo from G.L. Possehl, *The Indus Civilization: A Contemporary Perspective*, New Delhi, 2002, f. 182, fig. 10.9.

35. Woman and the water-mill (Mughal school, *ca.* AD 1602-05). Detail from a miniature in the *Nafahat-ul Uns*, British Museum, Or. 1362, f. 392b.
Photo from Aniruddha Roy and S.K. Bagchi, *Technology in Ancient and Medieval India*, Delhi, 1986, p. 19, pl. 10.
36. Women husking rice. Damodar temple at Kalyanpur, Howrah (West Bengal), *ca.* AD 1786.
Photo from Zulekha Haque, *Terracotta Decorations of Late Medieval Bengal, Portrayal of a Society*, Dacca, 1980, no.69, pl.XXXIV.
37. Woman spinning cotton on spinning wheel (*charkh* or *charkha*), *Maftah-ul Fuzala* (Mandu school, *ca.* AD 1470-1490), British Museum, London, Or. 3299, f.94b.
Photo from A. Jan Qaisar and S.P. Verma, "*The Miftah-ul Fuzala*: A Study of an Illustrated Persian Lexicon", op. cit., fig. 4.
38. Woman working on a cage pool (*kalaba*, or *preti*, or *prenti*), *Miftah-ul Fuzala* (Mandu school, *ca.* AD 1470-1490). British Museum, London, Or. 3299, f. 240a.
Photo from A. Jan Qaisar and S.P. Verma, "The *Miftah-ul Fuzala*: A Study of an Illustrated Persian Lexicon", op. cit., fig. 5.
39. A detail from a miniature "In search of Krishna" (Bilaspur school, *ca.* AD 1800).
Note: woman spinning cotton on a large spinning wheel, and the village men with cattle.
Photo from W.G. Archer, *Indian Paintings from the Punjab Hills*, Delhi, 1973, Vol. II, p. 190.
40. Women working with spinning wheel. Line drawing by Syed Mohammad, based on detail from a Mughal miniature (inset), *ca.* AD 1670.
See F.R. Martin, *The Miniature Painting and Painters of Persia, India and Turkey*, London, 1912, Vol. II, pl. 207 (left).
41. Men and women labourers working up to their kees in water. A 19th century AD Kashmiri painting showing cycle of the rice crop. India Office Library, London.
Photo from Sylvia Crowe and Sheila Haywood, *The Gardens of Mughal India*, New Delhi, 1972, illustration p. 39.
42. Washerman and his wife. *Anwar-i Suhaili* (Mughal school, AD 1597), Bharat Kala Bhavan, Varanasi, No. 9069, f. 160 (upper part of the miniature).
Photo from Rai Krishnadasa, *Anwar-e-Suhaili (Iyar-i-Danish)*, Varanasi, 1999, pl. I.
43. Washerman at home (Mughal school, *ca.* AD 1600). *Razmnama*, British Museum, London, Or. 12076, f. 48a.
Photo from S.P. Verma, *India at Work in Sculpture and Painting*, Aligarh, 1994, pl. xx.
44. A detail from the miniature "King Lavana visits a village", *Jog-Bashisht* (Mughal school, AD 1603).
Photo from J.V.S. Wilkinson, "A Note on an Illustrated Manuscript of the *Jog-Bashisht*", *Bulletin of the School of Oriental and African Studies*, London, 12, 1968, pl. 4.
45. King Janaka with ascetics, in his garden, *Jog-Bashisht* (Mughal school, AD 1603), Chester Beatty Library, Dublin, fol. 128b.
Photo from J.V.S. Wilkinson, "A Note on an Illustrated Manuscript of the *Jog-Bashisht*", *Bulletin of the School of Oriental and African Studies*, London, 12, 1968, pl. 6.
46. Picture of a disabled man (a beggar) supporting himself on hand-shoes (a detail from a Mughal album leaf, *ca.* AD 1630).
Photo from Toby Falk, Simon Digby, and Michael Goedhuis, *Painting from Mughal India*, Colnaghi, London, n.d., p. 23, no. 10.
47. Holy men (*ca.* AD 1580). Royal Library, Windsor.
Photo from M.C. Beach, "The Mughal painter Daswanth", *Ars Orientalis*, Vol. 13, Michigan, 1982, p. 124, fig. 10.

62. Holy men at Gur-Khattari. Detail from a folio from *Baburnama* (Mughal school, *ca.* AD 1598-1600), British Museum, Or. 3714.
    Photo from Hamid Suleiman, *Miniatures of Babur-nama*, Tashkent, 1970, pl. 29.
63. Mulla Shah and Miyan Mir (Mughal, *ca.* AD 1620-25). Bodleian Library, Oxford (Ouseley Add. 167).
    Photo from L. Binyon and T.W. Arnold, *The Court Painters of the Grand Moguls*, London, 1921, pl.xxxiii.
64. Dervish dancing. Detail from a folio from *Diwan-i Hafiz* (Mughal school, *ca.* AD 1610) British Museum, London, Or. 7573, f. 66v.
    Photo from D. Barrett and B. Gray, *Painting of India*, Cleveland, 1963, illustration, p. 101.
65. Khwaja Muinuddin Chisti and devotees at Ajmer (Mughal school, *ca.* AD 1660-70). Board of Trustees of the Victoria and Albert Museum, London.
    Note: dervishes in trance.
    Photo from L. Binyon and T.W. Arnold, *The Court Painters of the Grand Moguls*, London, 1921, pls. XVIII-XIX.
66. Dervishes and other celebrants trance. Detail from a folio of an unidentified manuscript (Mughal school, *ca.* AD 1600). Board of Trustees of the Victoria and Albert Museum, London.
    Photo from Bannie C. Wade, *An Ethnomusicological Imaging Study of Music, Art, and Sound Culture in Mughal India*, London, 1998, fig. 113.
67. Sages conversing (Mughal school, *ca.* AD 1650). The Hermitage, Leningrad.
    Photo from A.A. Ivanova *et al.*, *A l'bom Indiyskikh-i Pyersidskikh Miniatyar xvi-xviii vv*, Moscow, pl. 40.
68. A sketch by Peter Mundy of various modes of transporting women. After Peter Mundy, *Travels of Peter Mundy in Europe and Asia, 1608-1667*, Hakluyt Society, London, 1914, Vol. II, p. 192, illustration no. 12.
69. Women on a swing. *Miftah-ul Fuzala* (Mandu school, *ca.* AD 1470-1490), British Museum, London, Or. 3299, 290b-291a.
    Photo from A. Jan Qaisar and S.P. Verma, "*Miftah-ul Fuzala*: A Study of an Illustrated Persian Lexicon," op. cit., p. 32, fig. 20.
70. The spinning top (*farmuk* or *lattu*). *Miftah-ul Fuzala* (Mandu school, *ca.* AD 1470-1490), British Museum, London, Or. 3299, f. 212b.
    Photo from A. Jan Qaisar and S.P. Verma, "*Miftah-ul Fuzala*: A Study of an Illustrated Persian Lexicon," op. cit., p. 31, fig. 16.
71. The hobby horse (*kurisht, demin chob*). *Miftah-ul Fuzala* (Mandu school, *ca.* AD 1470-1490), British Museum, London, Or. 3299, f. 220b.
    Photo from A. Jan Qaisar and S.P. Verma, "*Miftah-ul Fuzala*: A Study of an Illustrated Persian Lexicon," op. cit., p. 31, fig. 17.
72. Girls playing with dolls. *Miftah-ul Fuzala* (Mandu school, *ca.* AD 1470-1490), British Museum, London, Or. 3299, f. 260.
    Photo from Norah M. Titley, *Sports and Pastimes*, London, 1979, p. 21, fig. 14.

1

Depiction of Ordinary Life in Mughal Painting

Art is a mirror of society. In other words, it is a visual commentary on man's life and his activities; and it is possible to reconstruct the history of material culture of the people in rich and vivid form from sculptures and paintings. In view of the vast store of information on our past that comes through sources like the written sources, we tend to forget that pictorial depictions long preceded pictographs and ideographs, the early form of writing. In pictorial depictions, upon stone in caves and rock-shelters, man has left unique records of how he hunted and gathered food. The discovery of Bhimbetka in India brought home to us how in his seemingly unequal struggle with nature man still found time to develop artistic skills.

The next stage was the attempt at a three-dimensional imitation of real as well as imagined life (Pl. 11). With agriculture and urbanization, we have statuettes of both the priest-king and the dancing girl from Mohenjo-daro. Plasticity and realism increasingly overcame earlier stiffness and survived the growing use of religious symbols when Indian sculpture began its history anew with the Maurya-Sunga and Gandhara art. The Gandhara sculpture produced the first known depiction of the Indian peasant at work with plough. Set under the benign gaze of the Bodhisattva, we glimpse here the play of genuine humanism (Pls. 1-2), and, by early medieval times, Yashoda churning butter became a favourite theme for the sculptor, delighting in the vision of the Deity sharing the small joy of the poor (Pl. 3).

In the meantime, without almost any previous warning, came the wall-paintings of Ajanta, with their breathtaking mastery of colour and line. Here men and women appear to us in devotion and at work, affected by all varieties of emotion. Despite much willful and natural destruction, enough remains of these paintings tell us about the real life of the times what we would have never learnt from any other source.

Miniature painting in early medieval times often suffered from stylization that limits the value of its evidence for the study of the people at large. Realism began to intrude in the work of the Malwa and Central India schools, but it acquires true dominance in the splendid Mughal school that developed under Akbar (1556-1605) and his successors (Appendix). Mughal art is essentially court art, but it is still one in which ordinary people are brought in to complete the picture. And, since every part of a Mughal painting aims at perfection in rigorously accurate detail, we have more intimate view of material life than we can get anywhere else in premodern Indian art. Mughal miniatures are scientific studies, and are particularly distinguished for artistic activity. Mughal artists' work is created in mind, and the artist was not a mere mortal instrument of divine will. However, it is true in the context of the artists of pre-Muhammaden India who worked for centuries to create religious art.

The famous Rajasthani and Hill schools are limited in themes and less exciting in detail, but much of what the artists depict is set in rural scenes; and these, too, are therefore useful quarries for reconstructing the history of the people. Of late, there has been an emphasis on the social and cultural history—a study of the people at the bottom of the society—but their daily life and work yet remain to be brought under full focus. These people, though constitute the largest section of society, never occupied a central place in historical works. Thus, their story largely remains untold. In view of the problems that are characteristic of research in Indian history, especially those relating to the source-material, the need of finding out new sources for discovering facts cannot be over-emphasized. Whereas the greater mass of textual and archaeological source-material available enables us to reconstruct a plausible picture of political and social life, the problem of cultural history is, by and large, still incomplete. This could be met by extracting evidence from sculptures, paintings, epigraphs, archaeological remains, artefacts, etc.

Pictorial representations, especially those bearing the stamp of realism, deserve utmost attention of the historians. They acquire greater importance from the fact that in them one has a visual information of what we may not ordinarily get in chronicles. In many instances, the descriptions are very detailed and frank. Even the commonest articles representing material culture are met with, testifying to the intimate observation of medieval painters. In the absence of textual evidence, nothing can be of greater value than contemporary pictorial records: sculpture and painting. Sometimes, we are at advantage over the textual sources, and the paintings are to be seen as documentation documents. Through this medium we find, in illustrated form, a variety of evidence that supplement or explain textual descriptions. The importance is still greater, when, as in the case of ancient and medieval India, textual evidence on common people is so limited. The pictorial evidence comes to us in the form of sculpture, frescoes, and miniatures, both in albums and manuscripts. Virtually, the illustrations have a role of authenticating history. These illustrate rural men and women in their daily life, and artisans and professionals at work with their tools and implements. Particularly the manuscript paintings provide not only a pictorial documentation of historical narratives but present the events with a vividness of details, which otherwise one would not have imagined or known at all. Fortunately, the Mughal period is the richest in this respect. The Mughal emperors maintained atelier employing a large number of painters. Consequently, we have fairly continuous record of their works. A good many of these have been lost; yet, those surviving provide us ample material for studying the culture of the time. There is need to resort to the history of painting to enrich the understanding of a period through its visual sources. There is no volume that turns to the illustrations to make the history of Indian people alive and largely, paintings are relegated to the connoisseur and to the privileged world of art.

Numerous Mughal paintings exhibit outdoor scenes (such as the remote landscape for background) that evince a scope large enough to cover the various aspects of commoner's life. The Mughal painter was not primarily concerned with the portrayal of the common people; nevertheless, the latter find a place in the composition. At times, the landscape background is replaced by interesting scenes of people at work, copied from real life. The picture, then, is wider in concept and it presents what impressed the Indian painter in a simple and realistic manner. The subjects treated include shepherds grazing their sheep, goats and buffaloes in the fields; stable attendants giving fodder to animals; labourers carrying building material; gardeners tending orchards, planting saplings and sowing seeds; peasants with ploughs and bullocks;

villagers harvesting crops and milling sugarcane; village women working on spinning wheel, churning, grinding the corn and drawing water from the well; fishermen and bird-trappers; singers and dancers in company; ascetics with isolated abodes; boatmen rowing boats; bookbinders and distillers and the like.[1] These miniatures are indispensable sources of information about the medieval life. As a matter of fact, looking at these pictures is like living in the times itself. Such genre scenes mostly appear in the background of the pictures since miniatures are usually part of historical narrative sequences or royal ceremonial depictions. The proximity of the people to the focal point in the miniature is determined by the nature of their functions. It is true that, in general, ordinary men do not occupy central stage in Mughal paintings. The cultivators or shepherds, for instance, are introduced in outdoor scenes on the periphery of the composition, often simply for the purpose of completing the background. A scene set in the countryside might depict a cultivator ploughing, or drawing water from a well. The life of the commoners finds only a casual entry in court chronicles; hence, full-page miniatures focusing on their life and work are few. Sometimes a theme may itself necessitate the inclusion of commoners in the plan. Outstanding examples are those depicting building activities, bird-trapping and hunting scenes facilitating, among others, the study of their tools and method of their work. In miniatures illustrating the construction of a fort or building, masons, carpenters, stonecutters, ironsmiths and labourers are prominently shown with their tools and implements.

In the illustrations of legends and fables, a painter had comparatively greater freedom to paint the life of commoners in their surroundings. "The Arab and the Baker" (an illustration from the *Anwar-i Suhaili*) is a lively bazaar scene (Pl. 6).[1] "Thief, Demon and the Peasant",[2] "Fisherman, Bird-trapper and Cultivator"[3] and "Women and her Sick Daughter"[4] are some other illustrations in the same manuscript showing ordinary life even more intimately.

Margin paintings are equally important as these contain some rare representations of bookbinders, scribes, painters, astrologers, gem-cutters, hunters, goldsmiths, *sharbat*-sellers and women distilling liquor, etc.[5]

It may be noted that in all the Mughal miniatures, the scale of drawing is very small, but the colours in the paintings are very accurate helping us to make out the material which the tools and implements were made of, viz., wood, iron, clay or stone.

Several miniatures contain portraits of common men. Outstanding among these are the works of Basawan,[6] Daulat,[7] Bishandas,[8] Bichitr,[9] Govardhan,[10] La'l,[11] and Payag.[12] These represent intimate aspects of ordinary life. The miniature "Battle between rival groups of ascetics at Thaneshwar" reveals Basawan's talent for portraits and his predilection for the life-like portrayal of ascetics, holy men, and dervishes (Pls. 51 & XVIII).[13] His other studies "Flute player"[14] and "Dervish"[15] show our artist's sympathy for the common people. He often portrayed them in isolated miniatures with striking psychological acuity. In another instance, a rare portrait of a Jain ascetic further reveals an artist's genuine passion for the study of Hindu asceticism and the Indian religious life.[16] In this context, the illustrations of the manuscripts *Jog-Bashisht* and the *Amritkunda* (*Bahr al-Hayat*) are notable (Pls. 44-45 & 52-53). These provide exceptionally individualized portraits of holy men and the characteristic studies of their practices, etc.[17]

Daulat was another genre painter and portraitist. Most importantly, he painted portraits of himself and of Abu'l Hasan, Manohar, Bishandas and Govardhan in margin-painting.[18] His "Dervish and a musician" is an intimate presentation of ordinary life.[19] Bishandas, acknowledged by the emperor Jahangir as "Unequalled in his Age in taking likeness" is important.[20] His work "Shaikh Phul at his place being visited by men and women" is a lively depiction of ascetic life. Shaikh Phul, a Sufi saint while staying at Agra lived in a single-cell house. People from all walks of life visited him. In the miniature, an old Shaikh is shown clad barely in the loincloth, and totally oblivious of the crowds of men and women assembled around him (Pl. XIX). It is thus described by Welch:

> Much of the appeal of Mughal paintings stem from their all-encompassing view of India and its people, as observed through acute eyes and perceived by minds at once curious, objective, and poetic. Jahangir, who directed this miniature much as Satyajit Ray directed the film *Pather Panchali*, brought to bear the same intelligence that sparkles in his *Tuzuk*. Pertinent "inconsequentials" engaged the emperor's, his artist's and now our attention: the crumbling brick wall beyond the inspired devotee; its mysterious door, leading nowhere, the beautifully wrinkled, baffling bits of cloth laid by the Shaikh at the edge of his platform; the seated figure (the devotee's devotee?) to the right of the house-shrine; the trio of shy but enthralled ladies in the distance at the left.[21]

We find that much of the appeal of Mughal painting stems from its sympathetic and accurate documentation of Indian life. Govardhan is another master painter who portrayed rural and ascetic genre with a degree of curiosity and sympathy unequalled until the early nineteenth century. Welch's observation on his work "A rustic concert" is important:

> With his favourite palette and dusty grays, Govardhan celebrated some of the pleasures of the road, perhaps in the coarse of a royal cavalcade to Kashmir. In the foreground, observed by the artist as though he sat with his patron on a platform in an improvised garden enclosed by a rustic fence, a Gorakhpanthi yogi and an attendant (the royal valet?) with a pet bird listen to a singer accompanied by a rababi. Beyond, servants set up the royal tents, one of which is red, signifying the presence of a Mughal prince; and on the horizon elephants are tended following the day's march.[23]

Welch has to say that Govardhan's studies of Hindu and Muslim holy men are among the highest achievement of Indian painting.[24]

Bichitr's painting "*Rubab* player, his companion and a peasant" (*ca.* 1620), which captures intimate aspects of countryside life, has drawn the following comment from Havell (Pl. 9):

> The subtler qualities of Mughal art are more conspicuous in individual portraiture and in genre painting.... Bichitr shows his quality as a genre painter in his picture called "The Tambura Player", for want of a more explanatory title, in Wantage Collection at South Kensington. It is a very piquant little scene, closely studied from life, in which a one-eyed[?] musician is singing with great gusto a song which excites the hilarity of his listener, the bowman holding an arrow in his left hand and apparently beating time with his right foot. The facial expression of both is admirably rendered, and the imperturbable countenance of the servant squatting in the foreground, with his bundle between his legs, is equally true to life.[22]

A number of unascribed miniatures depicting common people at work further show that the Mughal painters were masters in the execution of genre scenes.[25]

The lively effect achieved in these works vouch for the painters' keen sense of observation. Details are faithfully rendered and realism is achieved in the depiction of men and women and the objects complementary to the themes. Marek, Knizkova and Kuthanova observe:

> The large and small genre scenes reveal the acute observational talent of the Mughal artists and are an important (and frequently the only) source of information for cultural historians.[26]

On the miniature "King Oghus holds a feast in the Tent" from the *Jami'-ut Tawarikh* (1598) showing men slaughtering and skinning animals, the above authors remark: "The small scene is very life-like and an excellent document."[27] About another miniature captioned 'Sultan Ghazan Khan builds "Gates of Piety" and charitable institutions', they write:

> The miniaturist depicts in detail the various tasks of the workmen, some are sawing wood, others are mixing mortar, still others are carrying heavy loads, stacking bricks, building and plastering

> walls. One sees blacksmiths and carpenters at work using the tools employed at that time .... Its representation of this unconventional theme is simple and realistic.[28]

The miniatures "Water squeezed from mud for Chingiz Khan" and "Stones strewn on the dusty soil of the Camp" from the same manuscript illustrate the working people more vividly.[29]

Pictures of workmen are made with great accuracy. They exhibit the artist's skill in depicting dresses, tools and implements. Their faces are characterized, though they remain anonymous due to the absence of key inscriptions. However, in some cases, portraits of painters, scribes and the musicians can be identified from the inscriptions given on the pictures.[30] Their profession may be identified by their tools and the nature of work shown. Such representations are rare records of working methods of artisans and professionals. From this point of view, miniatures depicting bird-catchers, fishermen, bookbinders, artists at work, calligraphers, weavers, peasants, etc. are important. In no less than three paintings bird-catching forms the central theme (full-page composition), where almost all the devices and techniques employed in the trapping of birds are fairly shown.[31]

Folios depicting bookbinders inform us about their tools and method of work.[32] One such folio shows the method of processing leather used in binding books and albums. It represents an old man treating leather with a scraper. Next to him, another man holds a wooden clamp (*shikanja*) and two others are engaged in smoothing out a sheet spread on board with a heavy burnisher. On one side a youth is shown entering the scene with a bundle of leather sheets on his head. The next stage of the work can be made out from the margin painting of an album page of the early seventeenth century.[33] Here the bookbinders are shown stitching the folios of a book and filing the edges of the bound volume held fast between the jaws of wooden clamp. These representations suggest that different stages of the whole process required different skills. It may be fairly deduced, then, that this craft involved a division of work among artisans skilled in various departments of bookbinding.

Production systems based on division of labour are met with again in textile technology. In one painting, the process of making cloth is depicted in several stages (Pl. V). First, cotton is subjected to ginning by beating. The thread made from it is then dipped in starch to make it taut. The yarn is then dyed and stretched out on a frame. In the final stage, a weaver is shown working at a pit-loom and passing the shuttle across the warp.[34] Interestingly, the important stage of spinning cotton into thread is conspicuously omitted.

Bazaar scenes show fortune-tellers, bakers, sellers, peddlers, improvised stalls, and beggars seeking alms.[35]

A bazaar was also a part of the Mughal camp. A miniature of the *Baburnama* represents Babur supervising a camp where shopkeepers are shown occupied in selling articles to the camp-followers (Pl. I). It substantiates Bernier's account who gives a graphic description of bazaars set in Mughal camps:

> Outside this square are likewise pitched tents of their officers and troopers and there is a *bazar* in the form of a street, consisting of small tents belonging to the followers of army, who supply it with forage, rice, butter, and other necessary articles of life.[37]

Pedlars carried their merchandise in bags. A construction site shows sale of stuffs to labourers (Pl. VI).[38] The upper class people purchased their requirements at posh shopping centres such as depicted in an *Akbarnama* illustration of Fatehpur Sikri (Pl. 18).[39]

There are quite a few miniatures showing peasant life. Most importantly, the miniature 'Harvest scene' depicts the rural background (Pl. 16).[40] It shows peasants cutting crop, carrying it in bundles for separating grain from chaff by bullocks trampling the heaps, and finally winnowing. All this could still be observed in villages. Scenes, complementary to the main theme set out in one composition and rendered in good many details as in the present picture, is the peculiarity of Mughal painters. Another such representative scene laid out on a very small scale in the background of a painting "An expedition from Lahore to Akbarabad (Agra)" from the *Padshahnama* shows crushing of sugarcane.[41]

Village women are depicted in rural landscapes, or in the context of such themes as a water-mill in a hilly landscape, construction of a building, etc. (Pl. 35).[42]

This foregoing account is introduced here to bring out the diverse aspects of the theme as guidance for further study. In addition to it, the modern selection of the sculptures and paintings made here is meant to present various facets of ordinary life as seen by the artists over the long span of our history. We see here something of the evolution of production activities and techniques, something of the gender-division of labour, and something of the struggle that Indian people have waged for bare subsistence for so many centuries. We also see changes in ordianry people's ways of life, which form the core of true cultural history.

One remark, however, is warranted here: the picture of the common people of India which emerges from this documentation is largely connected with the working class. Both in sculptures and paintings, while their depiction is realistic, an idealization of forms occurs; but it never defies the historical and traditional character of the subject. It may be remembered that the details are faithfully rendered in them and especially great realism is achieved in the depiction of men and women and the objects complementary to themes. To sum up, it is only the visual records that provide us in detail the ordinary life and culture of the past in its purest form.

2

Village Men and Women

During the period, mass of the Indian population lived in villages, and the cultivation, the spinning and other domestic crafts, and rearing of the domestic animals were the major occupation and source of livelihood. The textile and building works were also other avenues which flourished in urban lands and populated cities. The carpenter, the smith, the potter, the washerman, the scavenger, etc. were others who formed an integrated part of the society. Undoubtedly, the life of masses of people constitutes a substantial part of the socio-economic system of a country and reveals the development and prosperity of the country-men.

A cultivator or a ploughman lived about half-naked. They lived a hard life, even bare necessaries of life being inaccessible to them. Here an observation of the Mughal emperor Babur (1526-27) is relevant:

> Peasant and people of low standing go about half-naked. They tie on a thing called *lunguta*, a decency-clout which hangs two spans below the navel. From the tie of this pendant decency-clout, another clout is passed between the thighs and made fast behind. Women also tie on a cloth (*lung*), one-half of which goes round the waist, the other is thrown over the head.[1]

Two illustrations of the *Anwar-i Suhaili* (1596-97) of Akbar's court, lodged at Bharat Kala Bhavan, Varanasi depict men ploughing the field; and the women carrying food and water for the men at work (Pls. 14 & III).[2] Ploughing was exclusively a man's job and their images corroborate Babur's description and suggest that there occurred no change in their life-style during Akbar's reign (1556-1605). In another instance, a miniature of the *Razmnama* (*ca.* 1585) depicts a village-man with his cowherd near the *dhekli*—a device employed to lift water from a well, or a pond to irrigate the fields (Pls. 12 & II).[3] He, too, is shown clad in one piece of cloth sufficient to cover his private parts. Likewise, the village-men shown engaged in drawing water from the well and watering the animals [illustrations from the *Khamsa* of Nizami (1595), and the *Baburnama* (*ca.* 1600)] appear scantly dressed.[4]

A miniature of mid-seventeenth century from the *Padshahnama* (Royal Library, Windsor) provides details of the functioning of sugarcane press in three separate enclosures, where a number of village-men are shown engaged in bringing the bundles of sugarcane on their head, cutting it into pieces, and feeding it into the mortar, and finally driving the bullocks to keep the pestle turning around. All the village-men shown here at work are half-naked.[5] Likewise, in an earlier illustration on the same theme belonging to the *Mahapurana* (*ca.* 1540), the men shown milling the sugarcane are similarly dressed.[6] A dispersed folio from the manuscript *Razmnama* (*ca.* 1600) is further relevant. It depicts the harvesters (Pl. 16). All the three men engaged in cutting the reaped crop, thrashing it to separate the grain, and finally winnowing the chaff are shown half-naked.[7] In numerous other instances, the men operating the Persian wheel, and driving a bullock-cart are in most cases represented clad in a piece of cloth, called *langota*, and a headgear.[8]

A narrow band of cloth wound round the head—a modest form of turban (a head-dress) appears as an essential part of dress, and even the half-naked villagers—and the labourers did not move bare head. They put on a turban or a cap.[9] However, the former was more common.[10] Most likely, to move around bare head was considered below a man's dignity, and the use of a turban or a cap was customary. It was common practice amongst both Hindus and Muslims. However, their types varied. No single dress was perhaps worn in such a variety of fashions as the turban.[11] A woman, too, was not an exception to it, and she had a long sheet of cloth (*chadar*), or a *dupatta* (or *orhni*) to cover her head.[12] One finds that initially the custom of covering the head denoted the dignity attached with a person, and with the passage of time it signified varied aspects of social life.

The shepherds, too, dressed up unlike village-men and usually lived half-naked. They are shown dressed either scantly or in a loin cloth or in short *jama* and short drawers.[13]

Could we infer then that the life of a village-man during the sixteenth and seventeenth centuries was bereft of even bare essentials of life. Rashid observes that earlier to it, during the Sultanate period as well, the dress of a man of lower status was simple and was barely sufficient for covering his body.[14] Ashraf has a similar observation to make on the life and conditions of the peasants in pre-Mughal India:

> As compared with them, the peasant usually worked hard unceasingly, almost day and night during certain seasons of the year. His exacting labour was shared by his wife and other members of the family. In return for all this labour he was lucky if he could obtain a square meal everyday. There are very few and very vague references to the life of the peasants, but it can be asserted with confidence that their lot was very miserable and they lived constantly in a state of semi-starvation.[15]

Of course, no change occurred during the Mughal reign, and the Mughal miniatures bear testimony to it.

Village women are depicted in fields, or in the context of such themes as spinning and construction of a building. These represent women carrying food and water, sowing seeds, etc. and engaged in different works at construction sites. A double-page illustration "Construction of Agra Fort" and another illustration "Building of Fathpur Sikri" belonging to the manuscript *Akbarnama* (*ca.* 1602-05) exhibit women breaking and pounding stones and bricks, sieving lime and carrying mortar-cement in pans (Pls. VI-VIII).[16] A miniature from the MS *Jami-ut Tawarikh* (1598) of Akbar's court, 'Sultan Ghazan Khan builts "Gates of Piety" and charitable institutions', too shows a woman carrying mortar-cement (Pl. 20).[17] Women were engaged in diamond-mining as well where they carried earth and drew water. Tavernier (1641-42/43) found women included in the labour force employed in mining:

> The first time I was at this mine there were nearly 60,000 persons working there, including men, women, and children, who are employed in diverse ways, the men in digging, the women and children in carrying earth, for they search for the stones at this mine in an altogether different manner from that practised at Rammalakota.[18]

In building work and diamond-mining women formed a part of unskilled labour only. At the working sites they are always shown fully clad but without a veil, though they always covered their heads with a long sheet of cloth called *chadar* or *orhni*. Their dresses show that they belonged to both Hindu and Muslim communities. A Muslim woman is distinguished by her *peshwazz*, a one piece garment reaching below the ankles and fastened at the waist-line.[19] The main dress of a native women was an *angiya* (a small jacket, a tight fitting bodice), and a piece of a long cloth (*sari*) wrapped below the waist line with its one end thrown over the head and shoulders. Babur also notices a cloth (*lung*), one half of which was wrapped round the waist and the other half covered the head and shoulders.[20] In some regions of Hindustan, particularly Rajasthan, a *ghagra* or a *lahnga* (skirt, a petticoat griddled on the waist line and reaching below the knees or up to the ankles) was a substitute of *sari*. The women labourers shown dressed in *angiya* and short skirt in the miniature 'Building of the Agra Fort' can be identified with Rajasthani village women (Pl. VII).[21]

A woman did most of the domestic work: she grounded corn, churned curd, fetched water from the well, and spun cotton. Additionally, she carried food and water for their men at work in fields. A Mughal miniature also shows a woman slowly moving behind the cultivator and sowing seeds (Pl. XIV).[22] Mughal miniatures exhibit women engaged in these everyday work. The milking of cows and churning curds was the work of women alone.[23] So also, to fetch water from the well for domestic purpose was a female occupation.[24] This practice is still current which tells us that these works are traditionally female occupations. Thomas Roe and John Fryer write that "Indian wives dress their Husbands Victuals, fetch water, and grind their Corn with an Hand-Mill, when they sing, chat and are merry."[25] A miniature "Ali Dost and Qambar Ali interpose for peace between Babur and Tambal" from the *Baburnama* (*ca.* 1598-1600), now in National Museum, New Delhi depicts a woman milling the grain with a rotary hand-mill.[26] An illustration of the *Miftah-ul Fuzala*—a Persian lexicon, belonging to the Mandu School (*ca.* 1470-90) – also shows a woman working on a rotary hand-mill (*dastas*, or *hath chakki*) (Pl. 34).[27] In addition to it, a seventeenth century Mughal miniature further represents a woman handling a corn-mill run by water in a hilly country (Pl. 35).[28] Judging by the practice still current in the villages, household milling of grain was an exclusive occupation of women during medieval times.

The spinning, too, was a female occupation. In the illustrations, the spinning wheel (*charkh*, or *charkha*) is invariably shown in the accompaniment of a woman (Pl. XI). A close association of this craft with women is noticed since ancient times. A rare depiction of women in the frescoes at Ajanta with textile tools (board-and-roller and worm-press, called *charkhi*) is notable (Pls. 4-5).[29] Here they are shown engaged in cleaning the weeds from the cotton with these tools. Horner finds evidence of spinning by women in the *Jataka*.[30]

An illustration of the *Miftah-ul Fuzala* (*ca.* 1470-90) from the Mandu school also represents a woman working on a cage pool and spinning wheel (Pls. 37-38).[31]

The miniature "Krishna lifting Govardhan mountain" from the manuscript *Harivamsha* (*ca.* 1585-90) is the earliest Mughal painting containing the depiction of women with spinning wheel (Pl. XI).[32] In other instances, the depiction of a spinning wheel under the thatched roof of a mud-house in a miniature of early seventeenth century, and the representation of a woman spinning the cotton from a spinning wheel in a later miniature of the Mughal school suggest that spinning was a common domestic work in the villages (Pls. 40 & XII).[33] A continuity of this practice is established since in numerous illustrations belonging to the Pahari, Sikh and Company schools of eighteenth and nineteenth centuries that depict women working at spinning wheel.[34] The miniature "From Gokul to Vrindaban", an illustration from the *Bhagavata Purana* (*ca.* 1750), belonging to Kangra School is of additional interest since it contains the images of village-women carrying the spinning wheel and worm-press on their head (Pl. XIII).[35]

The ordinary woman's occupations clearly suggest that her life was not confined to indoors. They assisted men in day-to-day work in addition to their daily routine work. The females in washermen's family shared equally with men the burden of running the laundary. A miniature from the *Anwar-i Suhaili* (dated 1596-97) is a fine illustration of it. Here, a couple is shown washing the clothes by thrashing them on a rugged stone slab (Pl. 42).[36] Interestingly, an event related to an episode from the *Ramayana* (*ca.* 1590), illustrated at Akbar's court, depicts a washerman blaming his wife for being away from home for a whole night. It is a lively picture and presents truthfully the living ways of washermen (Pl. 43).[37] A donkey, the most trusted animal to carry the loads shown in the left hand corner of the house, a large bowl-shaped earthen pot to hold water, and the washed clothes spread on a rope make the scene familiar to our times as well. The mud-house with thatched roofs completes the rural background of a washerman.

During ancient times, too, women did most of the domestic work and shared in dairy-work, handloom industry, and agriculture. A clay figurine from the Mound F at Harappa (*ca.* 2500-2000 BC) features a woman kneading dough or grinding grain (Pl. 22).[38] In a later example, a panel of sculpture at Sanchi (*ca.* 50 BC to AD 1000) shows women husking and winnowing the paddy (Pl. 24).[39] A woman pounded the paddy grains with a big wooden-pestle in a mortar. Here, two women are also shown rolling dough for cake. In another instance, a stone sculpture at Lingaraja Temple (*ca.* AD 1000), Bhubaneshwar, depicts a woman churning the curds (Pl. 3).[40]

The indoor life of women depicted in the Malwa, Mughal, Rajasthani and Pahari paintings further suggest that milking of cow and churning of butter were the household work of women during medieval and later times as well (Pls. 29-30 & X).[41]

Vijya Ramaswamy has observed that during 100 BC-AD 700, the women in South India played a key role in agricultural activities—seeding, planting, weeding and irrigation; in dairy farming—making and selling the curds, ghee and butter, and in handloom industry—spinning and dyeing, bleaching and washing of cloth. They participated equally with men as domestic workers and agricultural labourers.[42] Romila Thapar, too, finds women working in large numbers in spinning and weaving industries in Mauryan India.[43] Obviously, rural women co-shared with men in all major economic activities. Thus, women were an asset to the economy of the family. Nevertheless, an urban woman did not do much beyond her household tasks as mother, wife, or a daughter. No change is witnessed even later during medieval times. Rashid writes that the common womenfolk did not lead a secluded life. They helped their men in cultivation and in drawing water from the well (Pls. 26-28 & 41).[44] An eighteenth century miniature shows the continuity of the practice of women engaged agricultural labourers. It depicts women transplanting the saplings of paddy (Pl. 41).[45] A rare piece of evidence noticed by Shireen Moosvi also shows that during seventeenth century, women did actual cultivation in the regions of the middle Himalayas.[46] Thus, the evidence derived from the Sanchi panel (above) put together with the eighteenth century terracotta panel containing the depiction of women operating the device (*dhengli*) used to husk the rice,[47] would suggest that the village-woman was occupied through the ages both as an agricultural labourer and domestic worker (Pl. 36). She helped the man in a variety of ways, and cooked food and nursed children (Pls. 30-33 & IX-X). The clay figurines excavated at Mohenjo-daro and Harappa are the earliest known examples of women carrying children. Possehl writes that the figurines may well show the suckling child at a woman's breast (Pl. 23).[48]

The eighteenth century miniatures also show women as sellers or pedlars.[49] However, an earlier reference to it occurs in Tavernier's account. In 1641, he noticed at Burhanpur:

> From Brahmpour to Piombi-sera, 5 coss ... it signifies a great enclosure of walls or hedges, within which 50 or 60 thatched huts are arranged all round. Here there are some men and women who sell flour, rice, butter, and vegetables, and who make it their business to prepare bread and cook rice.[50]

Teenage boys, too, were an asset to the economy of the family. They were engaged in building work, mining, and souldering work. An illustration "Building of Fathpur Sikri" represents at least three teenage boys at the site carrying the building material (Pl. 18).[51] Tavernier takes notice of teenage labour engaged in diamond mining. He writes:

> The first time I was at this mine there were nearly 60,000 persons working there, including men, women and children, who are employed in diverse ways, the men in digging, the women and children in carrying earth, for they search for the stones at this mine in an altogether different manner from that practiced at Rammalakota.[52]

He further writes,

> When dinner is finished, each starts work, the men to excavate the earth, and the women and children to carry it to the place which has been prepared as I have said above. They excavate 10, 12 or 14 feet in depth, but when they reach water there is nothing more to hope for. All the earth is carried to this place, men, women, and children draw water with pitchers from the hole which they have excavated, and through it upon the earth which they have placed there, in order to soften it, leaving it in this state for one or two days, according to the tenacity of the clay, until it becomes like soup.[53]

Thevenot (1665-67) has an additional information to offer. He found little boys occupied in the work of souldering at Agra in Uttar Pradesh:

> This work is performed by poor people, and sometimes by little boys, who do it very skilfully and quickly, for a matter of two Crown for each tole of Gold; and something is also given to him that beats and flattens the Rods of Gold; ...[54]

Ishrat Alam has worked out that the Dutch sources of seventeenth century on various aspects of diamond mining show that the labour force included men, women and teenage boys. The Dutch factor, Pieter De Lange, refers that women and children (between 10 and 12 years of age) were employed.[55]

Admittedly, the teenage labour which prevailed during medieval times has flourished till today, though considered as a social evil.

3

Workmen and Professionals

A workman belonging to the category of an unskilled labourer, and engaged especially in building work, seems to have been the lowest paid person amongst the workers. The ordinary labourer is shown wearing a cloth-piece called *langota*. He wears a head-gear and sometimes carries a small piece of cloth to cover the back and shoulders. It shows that they were paid very meagre wages, perhaps just enough to live, and that even coarse cloth was beyond their reach. Comparatively better paid workmen, such as masons and stone-cutters, etc., shown clad in clothes in the same illustration, rule out the supposition that brief clothing might have been necessitated by climatic conditions.[1] Abu'l Fazl has mentioned the daily wages of the glass-cutters, bamboo-cutters, tile-makers (*khist-i tarash*), well-diggers (*chah-kan*), carpenters and those employed in building work as the lowest wage recorded, i.e., two *dams* a day:

***A'in* 87.**

ON THE WAGE OF LABOURERS

> *Gilkars* (workers in lime), first class workmen, 7 *d.*; second class, 6 *d.*; third class, 5 *d.*
>
> *Sang-tarash* (stone-masons). The tracer gets 6 *d.* for each *gaz*; one who does plain work, 5 *d.* A labourer employed in quarries gets for every *man* he breaks, 22 *j.*
>
> *Carpenters,* first class, 7 *d.*; second do., 6 *d.*; third do., 4 *d.*; fourth do., 3 *d.*; fifth *do,* 2 *d.* For plain job-work, a first class carpenter gets 1 *d.* 17 *j.* for one *gaz;* second class do., 1 *d.* 6 *j.*; third class do., 21 *j.*
>
> *Pinjara-saz* (lattice worker and wicker worker). First, when the pieces are joined (fastened with strings), and the interstices be dodecagonal, 24 *d.* for every square *gaz;* when the interstices form twelve circles, 22 *d.*; when hexagonal, 18 *d.*; when *ja'fari* [or rhombus-like, one diagonal being vertical, the other horizontal], 16 *d.*; when *shatranji* [or square fields, as on a chess board], 12 *d.* for every square *gaz.*
>
> Secondly, when the work is *ghayr-wasli* (the sticks not being fastened with strings, but skilfully and tightly interwoven), for first class work, 48 *d.* per square *gaz*; for second class do., 40 *d.*
>
> *Arra-kash* (one who saws beams). For job-work, *per square gaz* 2½ *d.*, if *sisau* wood; if *nazhu* wood, 2 *d.* A labourer employed for the day 2 *d.* There are three men for every saw, one above, two below.

Pl. I. A grocer's shop in a Mughal camp. A detail from a miniature in the *Baburnama* (Mughal, *ca.* AD 1598-1600). National Museum, New Delhi (No. 50.236).

Pl. II. Krishna and the Golden City of Dwarka (Mughal school, *ca.* AD 1587). A folio from the *Harivamsha*. Lower part of the miniature. Freer Gallery of Art, Washington, D.C.

Pl. III. Country scene. *Anwar-i Suhaili* (Mughal, AD 1597). Bharat Kala Bhavan, Varanasi, No. 9069, f.61 (upper part of the miniature depicting village men and women at work).

Pl. IV. A detail from the miniature "Babur visits the fortress of Urwa near Gwalior", *Baburnama* (Mughal, *ca.* AD 1598-1600). British Museum, London, Or. 3714, f.478a.

Pl. V. Weavers at work, beating cotton, dyeing thread, stretching yarn and working with treadles on loom (Mughal, *ca.* AD 1590). Johnson Album, India Office Library, London, Vol. 8, No. 5.

Pl. VI. Workmen building Agra Fort. Detail from the first half of double-page illustration. *Akbarnama* (Mughal, *ca.* AD 1600-05), Victoria and Albert Museum, London, I.S., 45 /117.

Pl. VIII. Fathpur Sikri complex being built. *Akbarnama* (Mughal, *ca.* AD 1600-05), Victoria and Albert Museum, no.I.S. 2-1896, 86/117.

Pl. VII. Workmen building Agra Fort. Detail from the second half of preceding illustration (No. 46/117).

Pl. IX. The arrival of Nanda and his family (Mughal, *ca.* AD 1585-90). A folio from the *Harivamsha*. Lower part of the miniature. Virginia Museum of Fine Arts, The Nasli and Heeramanek Collection, Gift of Paul Mellon, 68.8.50.

Pl. XI. Details from the miniature "Lord Krishna lifts mount Govardhan" (Mughal, *ca.* AD 1585-90). The Metropolitan Museum of Art, New York.

Pl. X. Milking of cows. Folio from a palm-leaf manuscript *Bhagavata Purana* (Orissa, *ca.* 17th century AD). British Museum, London, Or. 11689, f.1r.

Pl. XII. Details from a miniature "*Rubab* player, his companion, and a peasant" (Mughal, *ca.* AD 1620) by Bichitr. Victoria and Albert Museum, London, I.M. 27-1925.

Pl. XIII. From Gokul to Vrindaban (Kangra school, *ca.* AD 1750). National Museum, New Delhi.

Pl. XIV. King Dara meeting herdsmen in a landscape (Mughal school, *ca.* AD 1610), H. Kevorkian Collection (lower part of miniature depicting plough-men and a woman at work).

Pl. XV. Bazaar astrologer with his clients (Mughal school, *ca.* AD 1590-95). *Akhlaq-i Nasiri*, Prince Sadruddin Aga Khan Collection, Museum Rietberg Zurich.

Pl. XVI. Rejoicing on the birth of Prince Salim at Fathpur Sikri (detail from the lower part of the miniature). (Mughal school, *ca.* AD 1600-05), Victoria and Albert Museum, London, no.IS 2-1896, 78/117.

Pl. XVII. Babur surveys the mausoleum in the environs of Delhi (Mughal, *ca.* AD 1598-1600). *Baburnama*, British Museum, London, Or. 3714, f.370b.

Pl. XIX. House of Shaikh Phul (Mughal school, *ca.* AD 1615-20). Bharat Kala Bhavan, Varanasi.

Pl. XVIII. A detail from the miniature "Battle between the rival groups of sannyasis" (Mughal, *ca.* AD 1602-05), *Akbarnama*, Victoria and Albert Museum, London, IS. No.62/117.

Bildars (bricklayers),[2] first class, daily 3½ *d*.; second class do. 3 *d*. If employed by the job, for building fortress walls with battlements, 4 *d*. *per gaz*; for laying foundations, 2½ *d*.; for all other walls, 2 *d*. For digging ditches, ½ *d*. *per gaz*.

The *gaz* of a labourer contains 32 *tassuj*.

Chah-kan, or well-diggers, first class workmen, 2 *d*. *per gaz;* second class do., 1½ *d*.; third class, 1¼ *d*.

Ghota-khur, or divers. They clean wells. In the cold season, 4 *d*. *per diem;* in the hot season, 3*d*. By the job, 2 R. for cleaning a depth of 1 *gaz*.

Khisht[1] *tarash*, or tile makers, for 100 moulds, smoothened, 8 *d*.

Surkhi-kob (pounders of old bricks), 1½ *d*. for a heap of 8 *mans*.

Glass-cutters, 100 *d*. *per gaz*.

Chappar-band,[2] or thatchers, 3 *d*. *per diem*; if done by the job, 24 *d*. for 100 *gaz*.

Patal-band (*vide* p.234), 1 *d*. for 4 *gaz*.

Lakhira. They varnish reeds, etc., with lac. Wages, 2 *d*. *per diem*.
Abkash, or water-carriers. First class, 3 *d*. *per diem;* second class do., 2 *d*. Such water-carriers as are used for furnishing house-builders with water for mortar and quicklime, get 2 *d*. *per diem*.[2]

[d = *dam*, fortieth part of *rupiya* = R
j = *jetal*, twenty-fifth part of *dam*]

The table describing the wages of the men engaged in building industry clearly shows that the unskilled labourer was paid the minimum. The artisans and the skilled labour, i.e., stone-cutter, carpenter, and a mason, etc. had comparatively a better living standard. In the miniatures, they are invariably shown fully dressed in *jama* of short length, and a *payjama* (trouser) reaching a little below the knees, and almost not bare foot. Obviously, an agricultural labourer and an unskilled labourer belonged to the weakest section of the society.

The wages of the women and teenage labourers are not on record. The women must have been paid comparatively lower rates than their male counterparts, a practice still current in our times. Irfan Habib finds a woman heavily underpaid for her work and writes that the general underestimation of the value of female labour is shown by the fact that whereas, under 'Alauddin Khalji's (1296-1316) price regulations, the prices of "working men-slaves ranged from 10-15 *tankas*, the price range for "working woman-slaves" was only from 5 to 12 *tankas*.[3]

Pelsaert (1626) takes notice of the lower wages for workmen:

> For the workmen there are two scourages, the first of which is low wages. Goldsmiths, painters, embroiderers, carpet-makers, cotton or silk-weavers, blacksmiths, coppersmiths, tailors, masons, builders, stone-cutters, a hundred crafts in all ... any of these by working from morning to night can earn only 5 to 6 *tackas* that is 4 or 5 strivers in wages.[4]

Tavernier, too, takes note of the low wages of the labourers, especially those engaged in diamond mining. These were as low as 3 *pagodas* per annum.[5] Ishrat Alam sums up his observation based on Dutch Factors covering labourers and their conditions in the diamond fields: "their number was considerable and that they were paid low wages."[6] It corroborates De Laet's observation:

> The condition of common people in India is very miserable. ...Their (artisans) pay is very small perhaps 5 or 6 Taccas, i.e. 4 or 5 Dutch stuferi.[7]

De Laet finds the conditions of peasants equally miserable:

For the rest, the government is purely tyrannical, ... The condition of the peasants is such that they have to approach the chief man of their village (who is appointed by the king) and declare to him what land, and how much, they intend to sow, or where they will pasture their flocks and herds. When the crops ripen and are reaped, the royal officials are called, who take for the king's use about three quarters of all produce, leaving for the wretched peasant only one quarter, so that sometimes they get no advantage from their labour and expenditure.[8]

Bernier's (1656-68) detailed note on the conditions of the peasantry class is equally relevant:

Hindustan is badly cultivated, and thinly peopled; and even a considerable portion of good land remain untilled from want of labourers, many of whom perish in consequence of the bad treatment they experience from the Governors. These poor people, when incapable of discharging the demands of their rapacious lords, are not only often deprived of the means of subsistence, but are bereft of their children, who are carried away as slaves. Thus, it happens that many of the peasantry, driven to despair by so execrable a tyranny, abandon the country, and seek a more tolerable mode of existence, either in the towns, or camps; as bearer of burdens, carriers of water, or servants to horsemen.[9]

Bernier also finds lack of patronage to the artisans:

Workshops, occupied by skilful artisans, would be vainly sought for in *Delhi*, which has very little to boast of in that respect. This is not owing to any inability in the people to cultivate the arts, for there are ingenious men in every part of Indies...

Want of genius therefore, is not the reason why works of superior art were not exhibited in the capital. If the artists and manufacturers were encouraged the useful and fine arts would flourish; but these unhappy men are condemned, treated with harshness, and inadequately remunerated for their labour.[10]

He even considers the oppressed and miserable condition of the peasants and artisans sufficient to account for the rapid decline of the Asiatic states:

It is owing to this miserable system of government that most towns in *Hindoustan* are made of earth, mud, and other wretched materials; that there is no city or town which, if it to be not already ruined and deserted, does not bear evident marks of approaching decay.[11]

Bernier further takes note of the weakness of the Mughal rule, and high-handedness of the feudal lords in mid-seventeenth century:

There is no one before whom the injured peasant, artisans, or tradesman can pour out his just complaints: no great lords, parliaments, or judges of local courts, exist, as in France to restrain the wickedness of those merciless oppressors, and the *kadis*, or judges, are not invested with sufficient power to redress the wrongs of these unhappy people. ...This debasing state of slavery obstructs the progress of trade and influences the manners and mode of life of every individual.[12]

Tchitcherov concludes that the feudal system generated miserable conditions for the artisans. He finds that feudal authorities oppressed and applied violence to merchants and artisans in the 16th-17th centuries India. He writes:

Numerous source materials show that under Akbar and his successors the feudal lords oppressed merchants and artisans. Of course, this is only to be expected, for even though Akbar succeeded in resolving the contradiction between the 'general' interests of the feudal class as a whole ..., the contradiction between the interests of the feudal class and those of the merchants and artisans remained, while the state power invariably defended the interests of the feudal class.[13]

Forced labour or *begar*, for which no compensation was paid, too, was in vogue in medieval India. Irfan Habib observes that the zamindars were sometimes entitled to export unpaid labour services or *begar*, which was exceptional form of labour.[14]

It is notable that there were fewer artisans and agriculturists among the Muslims. In his description of population of Surat, Mandelslo says that the Moguls [Mughals] in the city were looked upon with more respect than the Banyas or Brahmins because of their religion which was that professed by the Great Mogul himself, as also on account of their capacity to bear arms. They had, however, an aversion to trade and business, and instead preferred service to any honourable profession, "for if they can but once get to be masters of a horse they ... fortune no further and immediately lift themselves to the service of their Prince".[15] Mohammad Yasin has similar observation to make: "Among the Muslim community there were fewer agriculturists, smaller number of artisans and a large proportion of household attendants of the Sultans and the grandees of the Empire."[16] He further adds: "The agriculture was least favoured by the Muslims and they dreaded country life as a punishment ...."[17]

It would suggest that the large section of the Hindu population living in villages was a source of labour engaged in agriculture and building industries, etc., and obviously, largely they were the oppressed class. Among the professionals, the carpenters, blacksmiths, wood-cutters, washermen, weavers, fishermen, and bird trappers, etc. hailed from both communities, i.e., Hindu and Muslim. Mohammad Yasin has to say that the artisan class was first to be converted to Islam and the royal *karkhanas* (workshops/factories) mainly depended upon Indian Muslims.[18]

The bakers, sellers and pedlars appear in bazaar scenes. In a market place, a baker is shown seated by an oven making flat bread.[19] The scene shows a large, rectangular masonry oven quite like what is in vogue in our own days. The baked breads are piled up on the top of it. Another man, apparently connected with the same establishment, sells breads, his stall being next to that of a vendor holding a balance (Pl. 6). It is a very typical scene and corroborates Bernier's evidence that breads were sold in the market:

> Bakers also are numerous, but the ovens are unlike our own, and very defective. The bread, therefore, is neither well made nor properly baked.[20]

He further observes that there are many confectioner's shops in the town (at Delhi and Agra), but the sweetmeats are badly made, and full of dust and flies.[21] Roe and Fryer also take note of the bread baked in oven: "...; the Moors is made of Wheat, thicker and oblong, be stuck with Seeds to correct Wind, and mostly bak'd in a Furnace, which they stick to the sides, when Dough, as we see Cow-Truds on a Mud-Wall."[22] They further write that the "Indian women make their Bread as thin as Wafers, bak'd on broad round Plates or Stones".[23]

As judged from the upkeep of their dress, it may be inferred that the petty shop-keepers and hawkers had a better life than a village-man or a agricultural labourer (Pls. I & VI).

ASTROLOGERS AND FORTUNE-TELLERS

A few illustrations show astrologers drawing the horoscope, or seated in a bazaar where men and women (both Hindu and Muslim) visited them to know their fortune. An illustration from the *Akhlaq-i Nasiri* (*ca.* 1590-95) of Akbar's court corroborates Bernier's description of bazaar-astrologers at Delhi. The illustration exhibits Muslim women clad in *burqa*—a covering from head to feet—flocking to the astrologer (Pl. XV).[24] Bernier writes:

> Here [at Delhi] too is held a *bazar* or market for an endless variety of things, which like the pont-newf at Paris, is the rendezvous for all sorts of mountebanks and jugglers. Hither, likewise, the

astrologers resort, both Mahometan and Gentile. These wise doctors remain seated in the sun, on a dusty piece of carpet, handling some old mathematical instruments, and having open before them a large book which represents the signs of the zodiac. In this way they attract the attention of the passengers, and impose upon the people, by whom they are considered as so many infallible oracles. They tell a poor person his fortune for a *payssa* (which is worth about one sol); and after examining the hand and face of the applicant, turning over the leaves of the large book, and pretending to make certain calculations, these imposters decide upon the *Sahet* or propitious moment of commencing the business he may have in hand. Silly women, wrapping themselves in a white cloth from head to foot, flock to the astrologers, whisper to them all the transactions of their lives, and disclose every secret with no more reserve than is practised by a scrupulous penitent in the presence of her confessor. The ignorant and infatuated people really believe that the stars have an influence which the astrologers can control.[25]

In another instance, a miniature, attributed to Govardhan shows the grey-bearded astrologer with an astrolabe and a water-clock. The man seated on his right is most likely a reverential follower of him. The whole scene set in a rural background comprising shady groves along watercourses suggests that the astrologers lived like hermits in a lonely place.[26]

A painting from the *Muraqqa-i Gulshan* lodged at Napstrek Museum, Prague depicts an astrologer at work.[27] It shows the time reckoning device, the sandglass, the ring-dial or the *chura-yantra* used to know position of the stars; and a disc on a stand containing 12 signs of the zodiac, and a book of astronomy.

Rashid takes notice of astrologers and soothsayers active during Sultanate period. People did not do any important work without consulting them.[28] Rekha Misra has additional information to offer that there were female soothsayers and palmists in the Mughal harem who forecast the future.[29] The fact seems to be that the male palmists and fortune-tellers were not allowed in the harem, and therefore the female soothsayers came into being. John Campbell Oman finds astrologers visiting men and women in villages and rendering their services door to door:

Only a Hindu fortune-teller announcing his advent to the women in the village. ...There he stands, smiling, and asute, experienced Brahman, clever enough to gauge the characters and, I should say, the weakness of the folks about him, if not wise enough to read their destinies in the motions of the planets he pretends to study. His services are soon in requisition, for who does not desire to anticipate the future? Yet not before the world at large can his secrets be revealed, and so the astrologer is invited inside the court, and there, with the aid of his astrological almanac he discloses in private the dangers, and with them the greater blessings, in store for his client in the years that are to come, and having worked upon her imagination, harrowed her feelings and excited her hopes the seer regains the street, with a small pecuniary reward and many solemn promises of further gifts when the happy events predicted by him shall have come to pass.[30]

People visited *faqirs* as well and consulted on matters of interest.[31]

4

Holy Men

The depiction of ascetics was a major theme of the Mughal painting. They appear in their natural surroundings in an unidealized setting.[1] The dervishes, *faqirs*, and hermits (yogis and *sannyasis*) are truthfully depicted wandering or in groups. We find that picturization of their ways and means of living, sartorial habits, etc. are in conformity with the contemporary textual evidence concerning them (Pls. 47-49, 50, 54-55 & 58-60). An observation of Ralph Fitch (1583-1591) is relevant:

> Here [at Allahabad] be many beggars [saints and faqirs] in these countries which go naked, and the people make great account of them; they call them Schesche. Here I saw one which was a monster among the rest. He would have nothing upon him; his beard was very long; and with the haire of his head he covered his privities. The nails of some of his fingers were two inches long, for he would cut nothing from him; neither he would speake.[2]

Edward Terry's (1616-1619) graphic description of the dervishes is equally meaningful:

> Among the Mahometans are many called Dervishes, which relinquish the world and spend their days in solitude, ... There are many other among them they call religious men, who wear nothing about them but to hide their shame; and these, like the Mendicant Friars, begge for all they eate. Usually they live in the suburbs of great cities or towns, ... They make a little fire in the day, sleeping at night in the warme ashes, which they besmeare their bodies. These ashmen suffer not the rasor at any time to come upon their heads, and some of them let their nayles grow like bird clawes, as it is written of Nabuchadnezzar, who was deriven out from the societie of men.[3]

Let us hear Bernier (1656-1668) as well whose description is even more detailed:

> Among the vast number, and endless variety of *Fakires*, or *Derviches*, and *Holy-Men* or *Gentile* hypocrites of the Indies, many live in a sort of convent, governed by superiors, where vows of chastity, poverty, and submission are made. So strange is the life led by these votaries that I doubt whether my description of it will be credited. I allude particularly to the people called Jauguis, a name which signifies 'united to God'. Numbers are seen, day and night, seated or lying on ashes, entirely naked; frequently under the large trees near *talabs*, or tanks of water, or in the galleries round the Deuras, or idol temples. Some have hair hanging down to the calf of the leg, twisted and entangled into knonts, like the coat of our shaggy dogs, or rather like the hair of those afflicted with that Polish-disease, which we call *la Plie*. I have seen several who had one, and some who hold both

arms, perpetually lifted up above the head; the nails of their hands being twisted, and longer than half my little finger with which I measured them ...

I have often met, generally in the territory of some *Raja*, bands of these naked *Fakires*, hideous to behold. Some had their arms lifted up in the manner just described; the frightful hair of others either hung loosely or was tied and twisted round their heads; some carried a club like to Hercules; others had a dry and rough tiger skin thrown over their shoulders. In this trim I seen them samelessly walk, stark naked, through a large town, men and women and girls looking at them without any more emotion than may be created when a hermit passes through our streets. Females would often bring them alms with much devotion, doubtless believing that they were holy personages, more chaste and discreet than other men.[4]

Tavernier (1641-42/43) also takes notice of dervishes and gives details of their clothings. He writes:

The only garment of these five dervishes consisted of three or four ells of orange-coloured cotton cloth, of which they made waist bands, one of the ends passing between the thighs and being tucked between the top of the waist band and the body of the Dervish in order to cover what modesty requires should be concealed, both in front and behind. ...The other Dervishes had for their sole garment a cord, which served as a waist band, to which was attached a small scap of calico to cover, as in the case of others, the parts which should be concealed. Their hair was bound in a tress about their heads, and made a kind of turban.[5]

Numerous miniatures show men and women visiting yogis, *sannyasis* and sufis (Pls. 61 & XIX).[6] The emperors, princes and nobles, too, visited holy men and their abodes (Pls. 8, 62 & XVII).[7] Babur puts on record his visit to Gur-Khattri in Peshawar. Gur-Khattri was a holy place of the *yogis* and Hindus who came from long distances to shave their heads and beards at this place. Babur writes:

I rode out at once from Jam to visit Bigram, saw its great tree, and all the country around, but, much as we enquired about Gur-Khattri, our guide, one Malik Bu-said *Kamari*, would say nothing about it, when we were almost back in camp, however, he told Khwaja Muhammad – amin that it was in Bigram and that he had said nothing about it because of its confined cells and narrow passages (account of the year 1505).[8]

However, Babur could not visit this place. Visual narratives of this event are known in the illustrated copies of the *Baburnama* (*ca.*1598-1600), lodged in the British Museum and Library, London (Or. 3714), and National Museum, New Delhi (No. 50. 326) (Pls. 62 & XVII).[9] Need not say that the association of these illustrations with the text of *Baburnama* is tenuous. Besides the point, the Mughal artist's work is a detailed and careful study of the ascetics of Akbar's period. These illustrations present a vivid picture of the yogis (the *kanphata* yogis), residing in group besides a huge banyan tree and a well. They invariably wear large, heavy earrings. Some of these ascetics put on long robes. Others are shown naked and wearing only loin cloths. They practised meditation and yogic austerities. The *kanphata* yogis had long matted hair and a flowing beard; and also shaven head.[10] The miniature also exhibits a disciple's head being shaved.

The yogic practices is the theme of the illustrations noticed in the MS *Bahr al-Hayat* (a treatise on the theory and practice of yoga), datable 1600 and preserved at the Chester Beatty Library, Dublin (Pls. 52-53).[11] Additionally, there are astray folios which depict yogis and *sannyasis* performing painful austerities (Pl. 59).[12] In this context, Bernier's account is important:

Several of these Fakires undertake long pilgrimages, not only naked, but laden with heavy iron chains, such as are put about the legs of elephants. I have seen some others who in consequence of

> a particular vow stood upright, during seven or eight days, without once sitting or lying down, and without any other support than might be afforded by leaning forward against a cord for a few hours in the night; their legs in the meantime were swollen to the size of their thighs. Other again I have observed standing steadily, whole hours together, upon their hands, the head down, and the feet in the air.[13]

Rizvi observes that yogic exercises are exceedingly difficult and call for great caution.[14]

Two illustrations on the theme "Fight of yogis and *sannyasis* at Thaṇeswar in 1567", seen in the *Tarikh-i Khandan-i Timuria, ca.* 1584-87 (Khuda Bakhsh O.P. Library, Patna), and *Akbarnama, ca.* 1600-05 (Victoria and Albert Museum, London) though present a violent picture of a battle, these represent the ascetics in a more realistic manner and greater detail (Pls. 51 & XVIII).[15] These portray day-to-day life of the ascetics, their sartorial habits, and the weapons wielded by them. They are shown armed with a sharp iron plate which has no centre.[16] They lived half-naked and performed yogic practices. A stringed instrument, called *ektara* or *kamancha* (or *ghichak*), and a fan made of peacock feathers to fan the spiritual teacher, or the deity appear to have been popular among the ascetics.[17] In both these miniatures, the residing place of the ascetics is identified with a huge banyan tree besides a small lake. They generally sported long matted hair and a beard. Smith informs that the figures of a few ascetics shown in blue (also in the illustration of the British Museum *Baburnama*) possibly indicate the body smeared with ashes.[18]

In another instance, the illustrations from the *Jog-Bashisht* (an abridgement of the Sanskrit text *Jog-Bashisht*, a work of 9th century), dated 1602 and belonging to Akbar's court show hermits besides their thatched huts in a solitary place (Pls. 55-56).[19] Their dwellings and sartorial habits, etc. make their sect identifiable and also the status of the *guru* (the spiritual teacher) and the *chela* (the disciple); and one may relate them with their mention in the modern studies.[20] Further the appearance of the trident (*trishul*), the drum (*damru*)—an emblem of Lord Shiva, and the conch-shell—a sign of Lord Vishnu suggest the hermits shown in the illustrations of the *Jog-Bashisht* belonged to Vaishnavite sect. Here the sages shown wearing the beads probably made from sacred *tulsi* plant (basil) further associate them with Vaishnava sectarians.[21]

The dervishes, the *faqirs,* and the holy men in general, wandered and lived away from the populated areas (Pls. 47-49, 50, 54, 57-58 & 60). A picture of a dervish by Basawan, a prolific painter of Akbar's court, is a lively portrait of him describing his peculiar dress, hair-style, and a sort of hunting horn, which he sounds to announce his arrival, or departure.[22] Amina Okada describes this remarkable psychological portrait thus:

> Equally characteristic of Basawan's aesthetic processes is the Musee Guimet's celebrated *Dervish,* a portrait of a given individual that the artist apparently came across one day and certainly not of a conventional stereotypical effigy of one of those Islamic mystics who abound in Persian and Mughal art. With a dog at his side—in Mughal India dog often accompanied ascetics and hermits during their long solitary wanderings and offered them considerable protection—Basawan's dervish, identifiable by the horn hanging from his neck, his pilgrim's walking stick (its extremity artfully sharpened) and the alms bowl (*kashukul*), belonged, most probably, to the Sufi order of Khaksars, which became popular in India.[23]

In it, the lively facial expression with intense gaze, slightly bent, lean, and emaciated figure imbued with gentle movement is unexceptionally naturalistic (Pl. 7).[24] The animal skin shown here suggests that dervishes used it as a mat or a blanket.

The sufis are generally shown wearing a patched coat.[25] However, this practice was sometimes disapproved. Rizvi writes that Miyan Mir (1531/32–1635) severely criticized this practice; and he himself wore a turban of coarse cloth and a *jama* (a cotton cloth).[26] A few known portraits of him bear evidence of it (Pl. 63).[27] Miniatures also show animal skin used as a carpet by the sufis and other holy men. Jahangir was much impressed by Miyan Mir and gifted him the skin of a white antelope in 1619. He writes:

> As it was reported to me that in Lahore one Miyan Shaikh Muhammad Mir by name, who was a Darvish, a Sindhi by origin, very eloquent, virtuous, austere, of auspicious temperament, a lord of ecstasy, had seated himself in the corner of reliance of upon God and retirement, and was rich in his poverty and independent of the world, my truth-seeking mind was not at rest without meeting him, and my desire to see him increased. ...This suppliant for Grace was taken out of himself by companionship with him, and heard from him sublime words of truth and religious knowledge. Although I desired to make him some gift, I found that his spirit was too high for this, and so did not express my wish. I left him the skin of a white antelope to pray upon, and he immediately bade me farewell and went back to Lahore.[28]

The *sama'*, considered as a source of inducing a mystical state of ecstasy, is the theme of a few seventeenth century Mughal miniatures (Pls. 64-65). An illustration belonging to the *Diwan-i Hafiz,* dated 1610 (British Museum, Or. 7573) represents two sufis executing a whirling dance in a state of acute exaltation while a third sings to the accompaniment of *rubab* and *daf*-players (Pl. 64).[29] The sufis attained a form of ecstasy in their dances, and under the influence of a state of altered consciousness are shown tearing off their garments and thumping the ground with their hands.[30] Rasid writes:

> "The frenzied lover bordering on insanity was aggravated when the sufi saints heard a line of poetry. Some went into rapturous ecstasy and gave a loud moan and departed from the world. Still some stirred with emotion began to shake their arms and legs. Under the influence of trance they thumped their hands on the ground. References are also found of the tearing of the garments in the state of rapture in the audition assembly.[31]

The holy men and the *yoginis* (female ascetics) were esteemed as sacred among the people (Pl. 61). They neglected worldly life and lived on alms. However, the Europeans were not impressed by them. Roe and Fryer observe:

> [A Fakier] is a Holy Man among the Moors; for all we profess that Srictness (for such it should be) they esteem them Sacred, and though before apparent Traytors, yet declaring for this kind of life, and wearing a patch'd Coat of a Saffron Colour, with a pretended careless neglect of the World, and no certain Residence, they have Immunity from all Apprehensions, and will dare the Mogul himself to his Face: Of this Order are many the most Dissolute Licentious, and Profane persons in the World, committing Sodomy, will be Drunk with Bhang, and curse God and Mahomet; depending on the Toleration the Mogul indulges them with, having been one himself in the time of the Contest among the Brethren so securing himself in till they had destroyed one another, and made an easy passage for him to the Throne; These People Beg us and down like our Bedlams with an horn and Bowl, so that they enter an House, take what likes them, even the Woman of the House and when they have plaid their mad Pranks, away they go to repeat them elsewhere. Under this disguise many pass as Spies up and down, and reap the best intelligence for the benefit of Princes that Employs them.[32]

5

Food and Use of Tobacco

The common people, both Hindus and Muslims, contended themselves with the minimum and the simplest food. The *khichri* (a mix of green pulse with rice cooked with water) was the most common dish and the only diet available to them.[1] It was unspiced and unbuttered dish. Abu'l Fazl writes that stable food of the generality of the people in the morning was limited to *jawar* or *bajra* flour kneaded with brown sugar and water.[2] Jahangir gives a graphic description of *khichri,* common among the Gujarati people, and has shown a liking for it:

> Of the food which is peculiar to the people of Gujarat there is the *Khichri* of bajra (a mixture of split peas and millet boiled together); this they call *Laziza* .... As I had never eaten it, I ordered them to make some and bring it to me. It is not devoid of good flavour, and it suited me well. I ordered that on the days of abstinence, when I partake of dishes not made with flesh, they should frequently bring me this *Khichri.*[3]

François Pelsaert (1626) while describing the status of workmen during Jahangir's time takes notice of their food:

> They know little of the taste of meat. For their monotonous daily food they have nothing but a little *khichri,* made of 'green pulse' mixed with rice... for their lean stomachs.[4]

The *khichri* was a popular dish. Thomas Coryat (1612-17) writes that the *khichri* was cooked at the occasion of *Urs Mela* at the shrine of Khwaja Muinuddin Chisti at Ajmer for five thousand poor men.[4] Bernier[5] and Tavernier,[6] too, find the *khichri* as a general food of the commoners including the foot-soldiers and the horsemen. The latter gives a striking description of it: For the horsemen as well as the infantry soldier supports himself with a little flour kneaded with water and black sugar, of which they make small balls; and in the evening, whenever they have the necessaries, they make *khichri* which consists of rice cooked with a grain of the above name in water with a little salt.[7]

Roe and Fryer notice that "Boiled rice, Nichany, Millet, and (in great Scarcity) Grass-Roots, are the common food of the ordinary people".[8]

People cooked their food on the fire made of cow-dung. Pelsaert writes that poor men burn cow-dung, mixed with straw and dried in the sun.[9] The cakes of cow-dung are in use even today; and the cow-turds on a mud-wall is a familiar site in village-side. The fire made of cow-dung caused smoke which enveloped the atmosphere. Pelsaert describes it thus: "Their houses are made of mud and thatched roofs ... and for cooking. ...Their bed-cloths are scanty merely a sheet, or perhaps two, ... and they try to keep warm over little cow-dung fires which are lit. outside the doors ... the smoke from these fires all over the city is so great that the eyes run, and the throat seems to be choked."[10] De Laet also notices the cow-dung fires in front of the houses, and the sheet of smoke in towns and villages.[11] Bernier's description of an event is relevant. He writes:

> But the greatest annoyance is perhaps in the evening when business calls you to any distance. This is the time when the common people cook their victuals with a fire made of cow and camel dung and green wood. The smoke of so many fires of this kind, when there is little wind, is highly offensive, and involves the atmosphere in total darkness. It was my fate to be overtaken three or four times this vide-spreading vapour. I inquired but could not find my way:
>
> I turned and roamed about, ignorant whither I went. Once I was obliged to stop until the smoke disappeared, and the moon arose; ....[12]

Ordinary men had a few earthen wares. A few miniatures exhibit the leather and earthen pots used to hold water (Pl. 9).[13] Earthen pots were used in other household works as well, i.e., cooking, churning, etc. (Pls. 26-29 & IX).[14] A pot with a spout was also common.[15] Jahangir notices a copper vessel used by Brahmins (Hindus) for drinking water.[16] Linschoten also notices the use of a copper can with a spout.[17] To drink water, the water is poured out from the spout, and the lips are not touched with the pot.

Of the lighting equipment there was only earthen lamp (sometimes wooden), called *diwat*, placed in the niches. It does not seem to undergo any appreciable change at least till the first quarter of the eighteenth century, quite in consonance with the stagnated life of the people of Babur's description (1530):

> In place of candle and torch they have a dirty gang they call lamp-men (*diwati*), who in the left hand hold a smallish wooden tripod to one corner of which a thing like the top of a candlestick is fixed, having a wick in it about as thick as the thumb. In the right hand they hold a gourd, through a narrow slit made in which oil is let trickle in a thin thread when the wick needs it. Great people keep a hundred or two of these lamp-men. This is the Hindustan substitute for lamps and candlesticks![18]

The miniatures show the *diwat* placed in the niche—a recess or a hollow in the mud walls of the thatched huts.[19] It is generally shown in the scenes depicting a gathering of the soldiers, men and women visiting ascetics, and an assembly of men enjoying music and dance during night. A *diwat* with or without a stand was the commonest and the popular lighting equipment in India at least till the first quarter of twentieth century. I recall the days of late 1940s when village-men and women used a kind of reed to light up the area.

THE USE OF TOBACCO

The use of tobacco, which was absent during Sultanate period, caught up with the affluent class during seventeenth century;[20] it also became popular among ordinary men. It seems that smoking was frequent especially among the ascetics, *faqirs*, etc.[21] as is gleaned from numerous miniatures (Pls. 61, 67). They sat in open, preferably under shady trees and indulged in smoking with *hukka* pipes. Manrique's account shows that tobacco became popular soon after its introduction in India in 1605: "He completed his speech by asking me to give them something wherewith to purchase tobacco. I gave him half a rupee, on which he said to me that it was a very small amount for four persons, therefore I gave them another half-rupee, which I should not have done."[22]

We know that the use of tobacco had become so popular that Jahangir ordered its prohibition in 1617:

> In consequence of the disturbance that tobacco brings about in most temperaments and constitutions, I had ordered that no one should smoke it.[23]

Need not say, tobacco was frequently used by the nobles. Thevenot (1665-67) finds that for the nobles smoking was a customary entertainment after meals.[24] Jahangir also puts on record that Asaf Khan, brother of Nur Jahan, was "without control in continual smoking of tobacco".[25] Mandelslo (1638-39), too, has a similar observation to make. He writes that Azam Khan, governor of Ahmedabad, was addicted of smoking tobacco: "Though the governor was on this occasion engaged in disposing off state affairs, writing and dispatching, he was not prevented from smoking tobacco, a servant holding the pipe to his mouth with one hand and setting fire to it, with the other."[26]

Roe and Fryer find the use of tobacco common among the ordinary men: "Boiled Rice, Nichany, Millet, and (in great Scarcity) Grass-roots, are the common Food of the ordinary People; which with a pipe of Tobacco contents them."[27] Tavernier took notice of women near a grand temple in South at Vijayanagar who for charity always keep fire to light the tobacco for travellers, and even lend a pipe to those who had no tobacco.[28] Both Hindu and Muslim were addicted to smoking. However, the latter were much addicted and frequently indulged in this luxury.[29]

Manucci (1699-1709) has to say that the consumption of tobacco increased and at Delhi alone the duty on tobacco exceeded to 50,000 rupees. He further says that the abolition of the act proved a great relief to the ordinary people.[30] Tobacco gained much population later during eighteenth century and both the men and women of high and low status indulged in smoking.

6

Dwellings and Hut-settlements

Hut-settlements depicted in the miniatures can be taken as representative of the medieval village scene. They represent houses with low mud-walls without ventilation and windows, having a single entrance with or without doors, thatched roofs, low mud-boundaries, bamboo fencing or shurb screens surrounding the open area meant for cattle besides shady trees and a well in the neighbourhood (Pl. 10).[1] The main building material was mud, bamboo, cane, reed, palm leaves and tree branches. The roofs of huts were supported by logs and covered with straw and a kind of grass, usually spear grass (*genus Stipa*). The rural habitation had minimal requirements. Babur observes:

> In Hindustan hamlets and villages, towns indeed, are depopulated and set up in a moment! If the people of a large town, one inhabitated for years even, flee from it, they do it in such a way that not a sign or trace of them remains in a day or a day and a half. On the other hand, if they fix their eyes on a place in which to settle, they need not dig water-courses or construct dams because their crops are all rain-grown, and as the population of Hindustan is unlimited, it swarms in. They make a tank or dig a well; they need not build houses or set up walls—*khas*-grass (*Andropogon muricatum*) abounds, wood is unlimited, huts are made, and straightaway there is a village or a town![2]

Ralph Fitch (1583-1591) during his travel from Varanasi to Patna also took notice of the ordinary houses made of "earth covered with straw".[3] A little later, Pelsaert (1626) observed that the house of the ordinary men are built of mud with thatched roofs, and they have no furniture except some earthenware pots to hold water and for cooking.[4] Roe and Fryer too find that the "houses of the poor are made of boughs or oleas of the Palmeroes, or leafs of teke, and thatch'd sides and coverings".[5] Pietro della Valle (1623) has mentioned the houses built of earth and thatched with palm-leaves during his travelling in Calicut.[6]

Tavernier's (1641-42/43) picturesque description of houses at Patna and other places is striking. He writes: "Patna is one of the largest towns in India, and is situated on the margin of the Ganges, on its western side, and it is not less than two coss in length. The houses are not better than those in the majority of the other towns in India, and they are nearly all roofed with thatch or bamboo."[7] Of the houses at Dacca he has to say: "... there is a succession of houses, separated one from the other, and inhabited for the most part by the carpenters who build galleys and other vessels. These houses are, properly speaking, only miserable huts made of bamboo, and mud which is spread over them."[8] Tavernier also writes about the houses at Surat. Here he finds the houses of private persons "constructed of reeds, covered with cow-dung mixed with clay".[9]

Bernier (1656-1658), too, gives a graphic description of the mud-houses with thatched huts at Delhi and the frequent destructive fires that engulfed such settlements:

> Intermixed with these different houses is an immense number of small ones, built of mud and thatched with straw, in which lodge the common troopers, and all that vast multitude of servants and camp-followers who follow the court and the army.
>
> ...
>
> It is owing to these thatched cottages that *Delhi* is subject to such frequent conflagrations. More than sixty thousand roofs were consumed this last year by these fires, during the prevalence of certain impetuous winds which blow generally in summer. So rapid was the flames that several camels and horses were brunt ...; for these poor women are so bashful and helpless that they can do nothing but hide their faces at the sight of the strangers, and those who perished possessed not sufficient energy to fly from danger.
>
> It is because of these wretched mud and thatch houses that I always represent to myself *Delhi* as a collection of many villages, or as a military encampment with a few more conveniences than are usually found in such places.[10]

Ralph Fitch, John Huighen van Linschoten, and Roe and Fryer have to offer an additional information that the floors of these mud-houses were spread over with cow-dung.[11] Manucci (1699-1709) also notices this practise.[12]

The human settlements established amidst the growth of shady trees is evinced from the Mughal miniatures (Pls. 10, 39, 44 & XII). The trees provided protection to men and animals from the bright sunrays, and a cool place for an assembly. Edward Terry (1616-1619) has noticed:

> Both in their villages and cities are usually many faire trees among their houses, which are a great defence against the violence of the sunne. They commonly stand so thicke that if a man behold a citie or towne from some conspicuous place, it will seeme a wood rather than a citie.[13]

De Laet has similar observation:

> ...; both in town and country the houses are surrounded by many trees, so that when we see a city from a distance it seems more like a series of groves than city.[14]

Thavenot (1665-67) also notices trees planted all around the villages which looked like forests or groves from a distance.[15]

Mandelslo (1638-40) and Tavernier (1641-42/43), too, recognized the significance of trees in Indian life. The former's observation at Ahmedabad is relevant: "Among other things I took particular notice of the Highway which they call Baschaban, and leads to a village six leagues distant from the city. It is so straight that it should seem they took a great pleasure in planting the trees about it, where-of there is a double row on both sides upon a straight line."[16] Tavernier's remark is more explicit. He has to say that on the sides of most of the roads are planted avenues of trees.[17]

7

Travelling

Ordinary men and women mostly travelled on foot and carried the load on their heads (Pl. XIII). The bullock cart was the main conveyance of the people at the bottom of the society. Abu'l Fazl (1595) has made a special mention of oxen of the Gujarat regions for their swift speed:

> Though every part of the empire produce cattle of various kinds, those of Gujarat are the best. Sometimes a pair of them are sold at 100 muhurs. They will travel 80 kos [120 miles] in 24 hours, and surpass even swift horses.[1]

Edward Terry (1616-1619) also notices the speed of oxen:

> They are drawn by oxen, one yoke in a coach, suted in colour, but many of them are white, not very large. They are guided by cords, which goe through the parting of their nostrils and so twixt their horns into the coach-mens hand ..., as that they will go twentie miles a day or more with good speed.[2]

Poor men and women ride the oxen alike horses. Edward Terry further observes that the inferior sort of people ride on oxen, horses, mules, camels, or dromedaries (the women like the men).[3] Peter Mundy (1628-34) also takes note of poorer women riding on an ox like men (Pl. 68).[4] Tavernier's (1641-42/43) account corroborates it: "Each one travels according to his status and means ...; and the poor, some on foot and others on oxen. The mother carrying her child and the father cooking utensils."[5] A description of a scene where people are riding on an oxen given by Tavernier.

He writes:

> I come to the manner of travelling in India, where oxen take the places of horses, and there are some of them whose paces are as easy as those of our hacks. But you should take care when you buy or hire an ox for riding that he has horns not longer than a foot, because, if they are longer, when the flies sting him, he chafes and tosses back the head, and may plant a horn in your stomach, as has happened several times. These oxen allow themselves to be driven like our horses, and have for a bridle only a cord, which passes through the tendon of the muzzle or the nostrils.[6]

He further takes note of the shoeing of the oxen alike the horses:

> In level tracts, where there are no stones, they do not shoe these oxen, but they always do so in rough places, both on account of the pebbles and because of the heat, which may injure the hoof.[7]

Thevenot also notices the practice of shoeing the oxen, especially when they were to cover long distances.[8]

An ox was the conveyance of the ordinary men in village and town. Ovington (1689) writes at the close of the seventeenth century: "They ascended the ox with equal ease as we do our horses," and "travelled longer and shorter journeys at a good, round, easy rate."[9]

Mules and donkeys, too, were used for travelling.[10]

Of the carriages, the commonest one was the bullock-cart made of different shapes and sizes, used for carrying goods, building-material, and for travelling.[11] Bullock-cart was in great use, and it could cover 20 miles a day.[12] The carts carried passengers and luggage as well. The mules, donkeys and oxen were also employed to carry the luggage and building material.[13] Camels were used especially in sandy regions for travelling and to carry the luggage. Abu'l Fazl writes that when camels are loaded travelling, they are generally formed into *qatars* (strings), each *qatar* consisting of five camels. The first camel of each *qatar* is called *peshang*; the second, *peshdara*; the third, *miyana qatar*; the fourth, *dumdast*; the last camel, *dumdar*.[14] About the mules, Abu'l Fazl has to say that it never forgets the road which it has once travelled. He finds it the best animal for carrying burdens and travelling over uneven ground. It has a very soft step.[15] The camels and the mules were the main animals employed during expeditions to carry camp-material and luggage, etc.[16]

Pietro della Valle (1623) gives a graphic description of the carriage drawn by bullocks:

> ... and that the oxen, which also, an anciently, draw the same, are fair, large, white, with two bunches like those of some Camels, and run, and gallop, like Horses, they are likewise cover'd with the same stuff, but beset with many tuffs, or tassels, and abundance of bells at their necks, so that when they run, or gallop, through the streets, they are heard at a sufficient distance, and make a very brave show. With this kind of Coaches in India, they not only go to Cities, but also for the most part travel in the Country.[17]

His description of travelling in a bullock-cart also holds our attention:

> Of the four streams which we waded the first was considerable; the other three came higher than the belly of the Oxen which drew the Coaches, into which nevertheless the water enter'd not, becausue their floor, and especially the wheels are very high: and you sit, according to the manner of the East, as upon plain ground, without hanging the legs downwards, but keeping them bow'd under you. For greater security they hir'd sundry men on foot, who held the Coaches on either side steadfast with their hands, that so in regard of their lightness they might not float and be carry'd away; and also to carry our bundles high on their heads, that so the same might not be wetted if the Water should come into the body of the Coaches."[18]

He further observes:

> The men who go on foot in this passage either strip themselves naked, covering only their privities with a little cloth, or pulling up their coat, which, as I said, is of plain linnen, and serves both for garment and shirt, and also tucking up their breeches made of the same, they care not wetting themselves. 'Tis certainly an odd thing to behold in this passage, which is very much frequented, abundance of people go every day in this manner, some in Coaches and Chariots, others on Horseback and on foot, men and also women naked, without being shie who see them; a spectacle, no doubt, sufficiently extravagant.[19]

Pl. 1. Peasant ploughing field. Detail from the Gandhara relief, *ca.* AD 200. Lahore Museum, Lahore.

Pl. 2. Peasant ploughing field. Detail from pedestal of Bodhisattva statue, *ca.* AD 200, Sahri Bahlol. Peshawar Museum, Peshawar.

Pl. 4. Women ginning with cotton press and separating seeds from the fibre with roller-and board. Detail from Ajanta Fresco, Cave 1 (*ca.* AD 500).

Pl. 5. Line drawing (illustration no. 4) after Dieter Schlingloff, *Studies in Ajanta Painting*, Delhi, 1988, p. 386, fig. 1.

Pl. 3. Yashoda churning butter. Detail from Lingaraja Temple (AD 1000). Bhubaneshwar, Orissa.

Pl. 6. A bazaar scene, Mughal school, *ca.* AD 1600. *Anwar-i Suhaili*, Chester Beatty Library, Dublin.

Pl. 7. Dervish (Mughal, *ca.* AD 1600). Musee Guimet, Paris.

Pl. 9. *Rubab* player, his companion, and a peasant (Mughal, *ca.* AD 1620). Victoria and Albert Museum, London, I.M. 27-1925.

Pl. 8. Jahangir visiting the ascetic Jadrup (Mughal, *ca.* AD 1616-1620). Musee Guimet, Paris.

Pl. 10. Hut-settlement. Detail from a miniature "The thief, the demon and the devotee", *Anwar-i-Suhaili* (Mughal school, AD 1570), School of Oriental and African Studies, London, (MS 10102).

Pl. 11. Working-men laying bricks. A detail from Bharhut Stupa, *ca.* 100 BC.

Pl. 12. Peasant irrigating land. Detail from illustration *Mirgavat, ca.* AD 1525-27. Bharat Kala Bhawan, Varanasi.

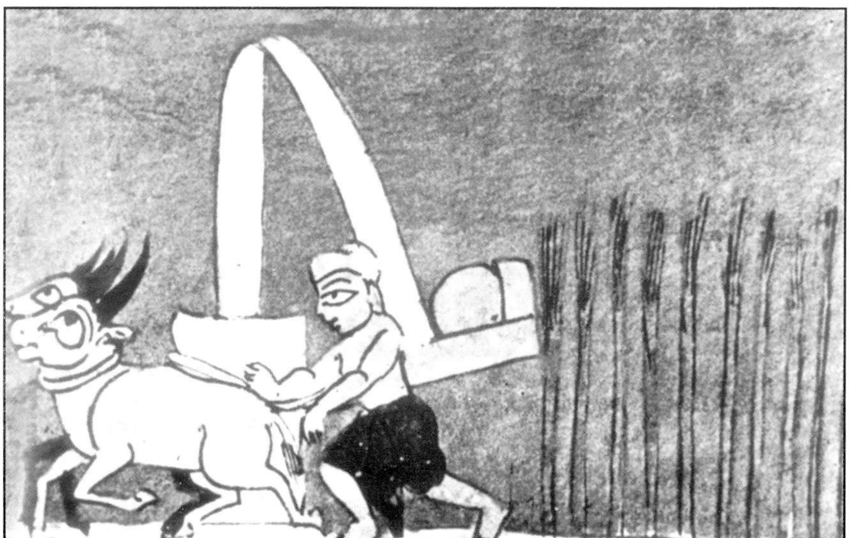

Pl. 13. A farm scene. Folio from the *Mahapurana* (AD 1540). Sri Digambara Jain Atisaya Kshetra, Jaipur.

Pl. 14. A detail from a miniature "A camel rider rescuing the snake from fire", *Anwar-i Suhaili*, (Mughal, AD 1597). Bharat Kala Bhavan, Varanasi, No. 9069, f.113.

Pl. 15. A detail from the miniature "A gigantic bird with a man in its claws", *Khamsa* of Nizami (Mughal, *ca.* AD 1595). British Museum, London, Or. 12208.

Pl. 16. Peasants harvesting crop (with sickle, threshing and winnowing). Detail from *Razmnama* (Mughal, *ca.* AD 1600). Chattrapati Shivaji Maharaj Vastu Sangrahalaya (formerly, Prince of Wales Museum), Mumbai, No. 43.35.

Pl. 18. Building construction (Mughal, *ca.* AD 1600-05). A detail from the folio of *Akbarnama*, Chester Beatty Library, Dublin.

Pl. 17. Building construction (Mughal, *ca.* AD 1600-05). Provenance unknown. Victoria and Albert Museum, London, no.IS 95-1965.

Pl. 20. Building construction. *Jami-ut Tawarikh* (Mughal, AD 1598), Gulistan Palace Library, Teheran.

Pl. 19. Building construction (Mughal, *ca.* AD 1600-05). *Shahnama*, British Museum, Add. 5600, f.372a.

Pl. 21. Masons building a wall (Mughal, *ca.* AD 1600). Indian Museum, Kolkata (No. 201).

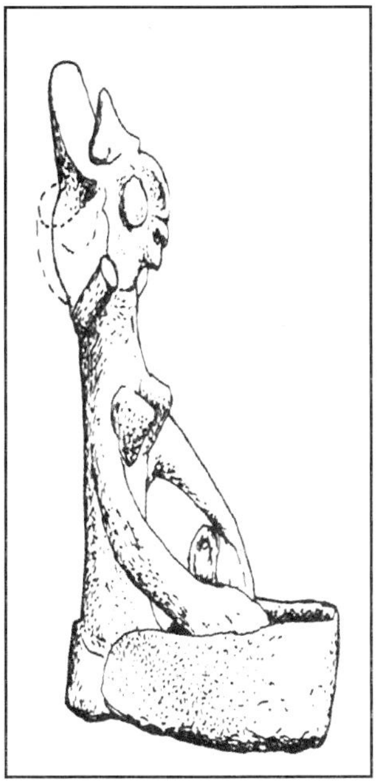

Pl. 22. A woman either kneading bread or grinding grain (after Vats, 1941). A figurine excavated from Harappa (*ca.* 2500-2000 BC).

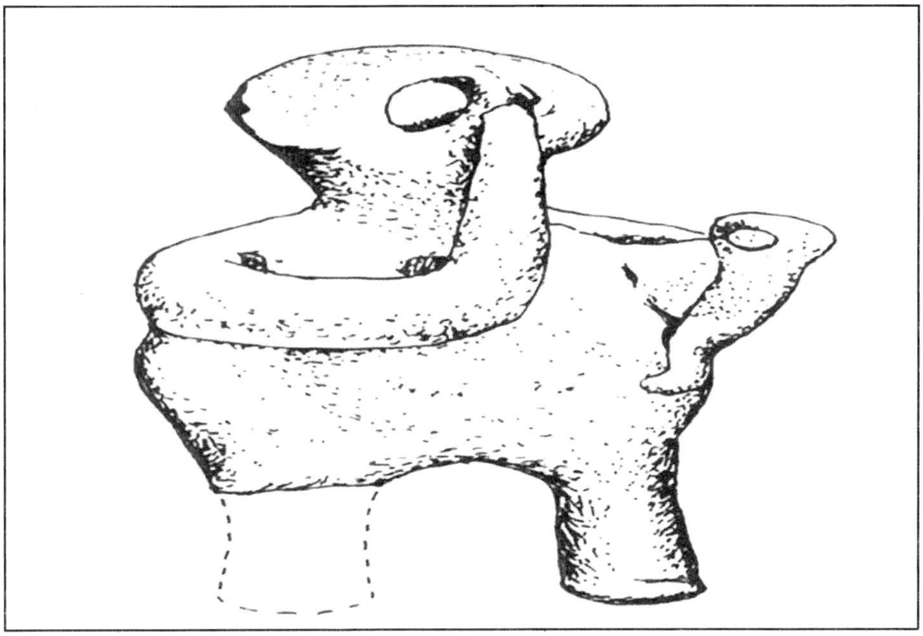

Pl. 23. Mother holding a child (after Mackay, 1937-38). A figurine excavated from Mohenjo-daro (*ca.* 2500-2000 BC).

Pl. 24. Women engaged in household tasks: husking rice in mortar with pestle, crushing grain with stone pestle, winnowing rice, and rolling dough for cake. Detail from Sanchi Stupa 1, *ca.* 50 BC to AD 100 (South Pillar of Eastern Gateway, upper panel on north face).

Pl. 25. Woman pounding grain in mortar (*jawaz* or *ukhli*). *Miftah-ul Fuzala* (Mandu school, *ca.* AD 1470-1490), British Museum, London, Or. 3299, ff.88b-89a.

Pl. 26. Woman carrying a water-pot. Detail from a folio from the *Mahapurana* (Gujarati school, late 15th century AD). Sri Digambara Naya Mandir, New Delhi.

Pl. 27. Women at village well (Mughal, *ca.* AD 1570). Detail from *Hamzanama* illustration, Victoria and Albert Museum, London, I.S. 1510-1883.

Pl. 28. A detail from a miniature "Shah Jahan visiting a religious teacher" (Mughal, *ca.* AD 1640). British Museum, London, No. 1920-9-17-0297.

Pl. 29. Woman churning curd with a churn-staff (*chaq, ravi*, or *ra'I*). *Miftah-ul Fuzala* (Mandu school, *ca.* AD 1470-1490), British Museum, London, Or. 3299, ff.89b-90a.

Pl. 30. Milkmaids enamoured by Bharata's charm. Folio from the *Mahapurana* (Delhi, AD 1540). Sri Digambara Jain Atisaya Kshetra, Jaipur.

Pl. 34. Woman grinding corn from a handmill (*dastas* or *hath chakki*). *Miftah-ul Fuzala* (Mandu school, *ca.* AD 1470-1490), British Museum, London, Or. 3299, f.119a.

Pl. 31. A woman tending her child. A detail from the miniature "A visit by the King to a family of outcasts" (Mughal, *ca.* AD 1603). *Jog-Bashisht*, Chester Beatty Library, Dublin, f.87b.

Pl. 35. Woman and the water-mill (Mughal school, *ca.* 1602-05 AD). Detail from a miniature in the *Nafahat-ul Uns*, British Museum, Or. 1362, f.392b.

Pl. 32. Daily life of women. An illustration from palm-leaf manuscript *Bhagavata Purana* (Orissa, *ca.* AD 1800). British Museum, London, Or. 116689.

Pl. 33. Daily life of women. An illustration from palm-leaf manuscript *Radhakrsna keli katha* (Orissa, *ca.* AD 1700). British Museum, London, Or. 11612.

Pl. 36. Women husking rice. Damodar temple at Kalyanpur, Howrah (West Bengal), *ca.* AD 1786.

Pl. 37. Woman spinning cotton on spinning wheel (*charkh* or *charkha*), *Maftah-ul Fuzala* (Mandu school, *ca.* AD 1470-1490). British Museum, London, Or. 3299, f.94b.

Pl. 38. Woman working on a cage pool (*kalaba*, or *preti*, or *prenti*), *Miftah-ul Fuzala* (Mandu school, *ca.* AD 1470-1490). British Museum, London, Or. 3299, f.240a.

Pl. 39. A detail from a miniature "In search of Krishna" (Bilaspur school, *ca.* AD 1800).

Pl. 40. Women working with spinning wheel. Line drawing by Syed Mohammad, based on detail from a Mughal miniature (inset), *ca.* AD 1670.

Pl. 41. Men and women labourers working up to their kees in water. A 19th century AD Kashmiri painting showing cycle of the rice crop. India Office Library, London.

Pl. 43. Washerman at home (Mughal school, *ca.* AD 1600). *Razmnama*, British Museum, London, Or. 12076, f.48a.

Pl. 42. Washerman and his wife. *Anwar-i Suhaili* (Mughal school, AD 1597), Bharat Kala Bhavan, Varanasi, No.9069, f.160 (upper part of the miniature).

Pl. 44. A detail from the miniature "King Lavana visits a village", *Jog-Bashisht* (Mughal school, AD 1603).

Pl. 45. King Janaka with ascetics, in his garden, *Jog-Bashisht* (Mughal school, AD 1603), Chester Beatty Library, Dublin, fol.128b.

Pl. 46. Picture of a disabled man (a beggar) supporting himself on hand-shoes (a detail from a Mughal album leaf, *ca.* AD 1630).

Pl. 47. Holy men (*ca.* AD 1580). Royal Library, Windsor.

Pl. 48. Two ascetics and a dog (Mughal, *ca.* AD 1580-1600). Royal Library, Windsor.

Pl. 49. Shepherd offering flower to a holy man (Mughal, *ca.* AD 1620). Johnson Album, India Office Library, London, Vol. 22, no.13.

Pl. 50. Hindu holy men (Mughal, *ca.* AD 1625). Private Collection, courtesy of the Fogg Art Museum.

Pl. 52. Yogic posture. Folio from a *Bahr al-Hayat* manuscript (Mughal, *ca.* AD 1600). Chester Beatty Library, Dublin.

Pl. 51. A detail from the miniature "Battle between the rival groups of sannyasis" (Mughal, *ca.* AD 1584-87), *Tarikh-i Khandan-i Timuria*, Khuda Bakhsh O.P. Library, Patna, f.322a.

Pl. 53. Yogic posture. Folio from a *Bahr al-Hayat* manuscript (Mughal, *ca.* AD 1600). Chester Beatty Library, Dublin.

Pl. 54. Detail from a miniature "An episode during a hunt" (Mughal, *ca.* AD 1600). From a private collection.

Pl. 55. A meeting between two ascetics, *Jog-Bashisht* (Mughal school, AD 1603).

Pl. 56. Shiva and Parvati appearing to the sage Vashisht, *Jog-Bashisht* (Mughal school, AD 1603).

Pl. 57. Faqirs resting under trees (Mughal, *ca.* AD 1650). Collection of Baron Maurice Rothschild, Paris.

Pl. 58. Ascetics. Detail from an album page from the Berlin Album (Mughal school, *ca.* AD 1610). Staatschibilothek Preussicher Kulturbesitz, Berlin [MS A117, f.6b].

Pl. 59. Ascetics. Mughal school, *ca.* AD 1645. Linden Museum, Stuttgart (SA 374261).

Pl. 60. A gathering of mystics. Mughal school, *ca.* AD 1650-55. Collection of Professor William Rothenstein.

Pl. 62. Holy men at Gur-Khattari. Detail from a folio from *Baburnama* (Mughal school, *ca.* AD 1598-1600), British Museum, Or. 3714.

Pl. 61. A woman visiting a yogni, Mughal (Delhi), *ca.* AD 1800. Virginia Museum of Fine Arts, Gift of Mr. John D. Archbold, 83.123.

Pl. 63. Mulla Shah and Miyan Mir (Mughal, *ca.* AD 1620-25). Bodleian Library, Oxford (Ouseley Add. 167).

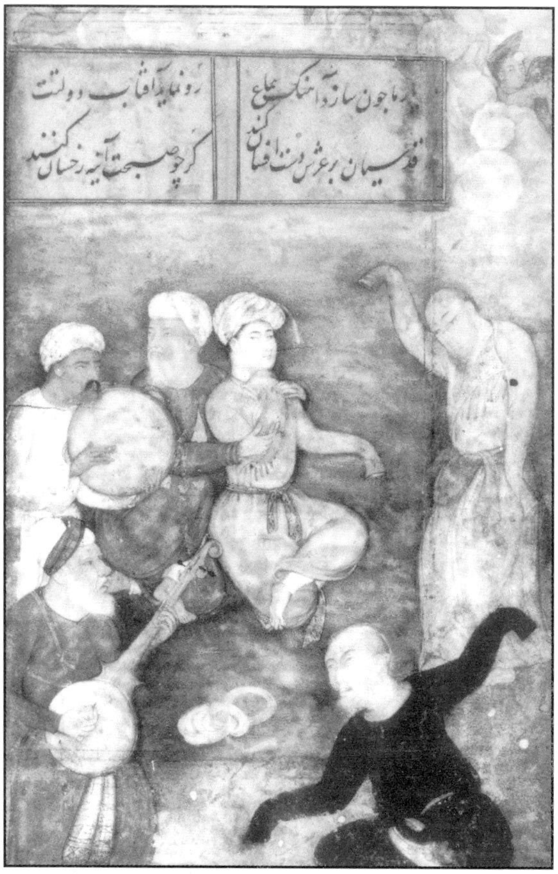

Pl. 64. Dervish dancing. Detail from a folio from *Diwan-i Hafiz* (Mughal school, *ca.* AD 1610). British Museum, London, Or. 7573, f.66v.

Pl. 65. Khwaja Muinuddin Chisti and devotees at Ajmer (Mughal school, *ca.* AD 1660-70). Board of Trustees of the Victoria and Albert Museum, London.

Pl. 68. A sketch by Peter Mundy of various modes of transporting women. After Peter Mundy, *Travels of Peter Mundy in Europe and Asia, 1608-1667*, Hakluyt Society, London, 1914, Vol. II, p. 192, illustration no. 12.

Pl. 66. Dervishes and other celebrants trance. Detail from a folio of an unidentified manuscript (Mughal school, *ca.* AD 1600). Board of Trustees of the Victoria and Albert Museum, London.

Pl. 67. Sages conversing (Mughal school, *ca.* AD 1650). The Hermitage, Leningrad.

Pl. 69. Women on a swing. *Miftah-ul Fuzala* (Mandu school, *ca.* AD 1470-1490), British Museum, London, Or. 3299, 290b-291a.

Pl. 70. The spinning top (*farmuk*, or *lattu*). *Miftah-ul Fuzala* (Mandu school, *ca.* AD 1470-1490), British Museum, London, Or. 3299, f.212b.

Pl. 72. Girls playing with dolls. *Miftah-ul Fuzala* (Mandu school, *ca.* AD 1470-1490), British Museum, London, Or. 3299, f.260.

Pl. 71. The hobby horse (*kurisht, demin chob*). *Miftah-ul Fuzala* (Mandu school, *ca.* AD 1470-1490), British Museum, London, Or. 3299, f.220b.

Epilogue

Pictorial art, though important, and sometimes indispensable in constructing history of the past yet remains to be examined. Mughal painters practised a straightforward realism in their art, and successfully explored individuality of the figures. Their images in the miniatures are fully authentic and with no sign of idealization. For the Mughal painter, painting was a way of exploring the external world of reality. The 'realism' evinced in the Mughal painters' work lend the Mughal pictures a quality of biographical record. It is especially true regarding the genre scenes from everyday life.

Pictorial representations, especially those bearing the stamp of realism, deserve utmost attention of the historians. They acquire greater importance from the fact that in them one has a visual information of what we may not ordinarily get in chronicles. In many instances the descriptions are very detailed and frank.

It is true that Mughal painting despite being urban in character, occasionally affords glimpses of common life. Mughal painting is always descriptive and secular, and there are excellent documentary records of the life at the Mughal court with glimpses of the larger social life away from the courts. However, the fact remains that the common people and the tribes did matter but little in the medieval feudal society of India.

Our study shows that village men and women had a hard time and even the bare necessities, that is, food, shelter and clothing were scarce in their life. A ploughman, and an unskilled labour who worked on a construction site lived half-naked in low mud-huts with thatched roofs. He survived on *khichri*—a poor man's diet. Women did most of the domestic work, i.e., cooking, milling the grain, husking the rice, churning the butter in addition to nursing of children. They fetched water for cooking, etc. from the well, tank, river, etc., carried food and water for men at work in fields, and in building industries they were engaged as labourer to pound the bricks, and to carry mortar cement in pans on their head. Both Hindu and Muslim women worked on construction site. Their wages were low. Even today, a woman is not paid equal wages to the men, nor does she get the position they felt she deserves at her place of work.

An ordinary woman did not observe *parda*, but always used the lapel of their *sari* or a *dupatta* to cover their head. A women's life was not secluded and she worked in the fields with men, collected cow-dung and wood for fuel and joined the labour force in diamond mining, and building industry. These women crossed the gender line and were sociable. However, the

Muslim women kept themselves in veil even when working on the construction sites, or meeting the fortune-tellers and visiting the *faqirs*, etc.

Teenage labour too was in vogue during medieval times and the teenage boys were employed in diamond mining industry and building industry, etc. This necessary evil is yet to be eradicated from our modern society.

Artisans, too, were a miserable lot due to low wages, and also the unkind treatment given to them from the ruling and affluent class.

Forced labour (*begar*), too, was prevalent in the medieval feudal society of India.

Most likely, the vast mass of the people was grieved by poverty.

Fortune-tellers commonly seen in the bazaars were visited by both men and women; and especially the latter flocked around them in groups to know their fortune.

Ascetics and *faqirs*, etc. who wandered from place to place and lived in a secluded place were highly esteemed by people. They visited them to seek their blessings. However, Europeans were not impressed and considered them hypocrite. A good number of illustrations depicting yogis and *sannyasis* represent them practising severe austerities. Further, the life of sufis and dervishes is vividly portrayed, and the *sama'* (sufis in ecstasy) is the theme of a few Mughal paintings.

The women, too, are known to have led the life of an ascetic and soothed the people visiting them (Pl. 61).

Most likely, the use of tobacco had become common during the medieval times, and the ascetics, etc. are shown smoking *hukka*-pipe, or a *gurhgurhi*.

The mud-huts with thatched roof represented the dwellings of common people. The walls plastered with mud and cow-dung were low and without ventilation. People had no furniture and slept on floor. They had a few earthen pots for cooking and to keep water. An earthen lamp, called *diwat*, was the only lighting equipment. The shady trees commonly seen around the hut-settlements protected the men and animal from the scorching sun.

Europeans who travelled into different parts of the country have made similar observations regarding the dwellings of ordinary men. The houses of the commonest imperial servants, too, were built of mud and thatched with straw. Here Bernier's (1656-68) observation is interestnig to consider: "It is because of these wretched mud and thatch houses that I always represent to myself Delhi as a collection of villages."

A road-side gathering with a singer or a musician was a good pastime. A tambourin (the *daf*, or the *chang*), or a flute (the *alghoza*, or the *bansuri*), a drum (the *dhol*), and finally a stringed-instrument (the *ektara*, or *kamancha*, or the *rubab*) were the modest musical instruments played by them (Pls. 9 & 64-65). The jugglers' tricks, popular melodies sung on the swings, gatherings with folk-dancers and singers on festive occasions, etc. increased the pleasing moments in the everyday life of the people, in general (Pl. 69). The children played with spinning top or a yoyo (*farmuk*) and the hobby horses in the form of sticks ridden by them (Pls. 70-71). The girls played with dolls (Pl. 72).

One finds the dogs and the caged-birds, generally a parrot, as their pet in the accompaniment of the commoners. A dog appears as a needed companion of a wandering yogi or a dervish.

Ordinary men travelled on foot, and carried the load on their head. Sometimes, they maintained mules, donkeys and oxen as part of their professional tasks to carry loads and for travelling as well. A poor woman often travelled on bullock. For long distance journey, a bullock cart was the conveyance of the commoners. Mules were also used as mounts and as pack-and-draught animals.

The number of poverty-stricken men and women was notable. We see the poor, indigent and the disabled people thronging outside the palaces, shrines and tombs, etc. begging alms (Pls. 46 & XVI). Begging itself was in vogue, adopted as an occupation. The beggars seeking alms roamed through the bazaars and streets (Pl. 6).

Babur's observations about Hindustan and its people made in his *Memoirs* (1530) is almost appropriate for the whole Mughal period, and the pictorial evidence bear no trace of a notable change in the life and conditions of the people, in general. It hints at the stagnated life of men and women who for centuries laboured for livelihood and lived oppressed by poverty. Such was the village life five hundred years ago; such it is today, and there is not one of the equipments, gadgets, and utensils represented which is not still in use.

The foregoing account of the life of ordinary people portrayed in paintings, especially from the Mughal school, might be of some value to social historians. Here the modest selection of the examples from the Indian sculpture and painting is meant to present various facets of ordinary life as seen by the artists over the long span of our history.

Notes

DEPICTION OF ORDINARY LIFE IN MUGHAL PAINTING

1. For reproduction, see Linda Leach, "Life at Court" in *Image of Man: The Indian Perception of the Universe through 2000 years of Painting and Sculpture*, Delhi, 1982, p. 160, fig. 228.
2. Reproduced and described: S.C. Welch, *India: Art and Culture, 1300-1900*, New York, 1985, no. 93a, pp. 154-55, pl. on p. 156.
3. Reproduced and described: Rai Krishnadasa, *Anwar-e-Suhaili (Iyar-i-Danish)*, Varanasi, 1999, p. 73, pl. D ("A city is shown at a distance at the top of this painting in a traditional manner of other Mughal paintings of the same period. The artist has been extremely successful in displaying people of different professionals actively engaged in their work. Everyone in this painting has been shown in realistic movements. The ploughman and the two fishermen proceeding in opposite directions from one another, serve to highlight the main figure of fisherman catching fishes. The artist has very faithfully captured the landscape of a typical countryside in this painting").
4. Ibid., pp. 78-9, pl. J ("On the varandah, a sick girl named Muhasti is shown reclining on a bed. Her mother is shown standing near the gate. ...The lower part of this painting shows a rustic scene—a group of cows and buffaloes either standing or seated or drinking water from a pond").
   See also p. 76, pl. H ("The upper part includes a city in distance along with a cultivable land in the middle. The land is being cultivated by a farmer while his wife brings meal for him carrying it on her head").
5. See *Jahangir Album*, Staasbibliothek zu Berlin—Preussischer Kulturbestiz, Orientabteilung, ff.7a, 18a, 21b and 24a (E. Kuhnel and H. Goetz, *Indian Book Painting*, London, 1926, pls.19 (top), 20, 23-4 and 26); 'Prince Salim with a cup of wine', Naprstek Library, Prague (L. Hajek, *Indian Miniatures of the Mughal School*, London, 1960, pl.76, no.15, pls.10 and 18); 'Preparation of Books', Freer Gallery of Art, Washington, D.C., no.54.116 (Esin Atil, *The Brush of Masters: Drawings from Iran and India*, Washington, 1978, no.63, pp. 106-07); *Muraqqa'-i Gulshan*, Gulistan Palace Museum, Teheran, ff.44, 68, 140 (Y.A. Godard, "Les Marges du Murakka' Gulshan", *Athar-e-Iran*, I, Haarlem, 1936, figs.4, 9-14, 20-1).
6. See S.P. Verma, *Mughal Painters and Their Work: A Biographical Survey and Comprehensive Catalogue*, New Delhi, 1994, pp. 87-93, nos. 63, 75, 92-3, 95, 106-07, 118 and 120.
7. Ibid., p. 128, nos. 8-10.
8. Ibid., pp. 111-114, nos. 1, 20, 35.
9. Ibid., pp. 106-09, nos. 7-9, 24, 34.
10. Ibid., pp. 162-66, nos. 14, 18-9, 23, 38-9, 49, 50, 55, 57, 58.
11. Ibid., p. 231, nos. 135, 138.

12. Ibid., pp. 327-29, nos. 1, 5-6, 18.
13. Reproduced and described: Geeti Sen, *Paintings from the Akbarnama*, New Delhi, 1984, pp. 105-09, pls. 42-5.
14. Reproduced and described: Amina Okada, *Imperial Mughal Painters*, Flammarion, no date, p. 91, fig. 91; See also another lyrical portrait of a musician by Mansur (*ca.* 1600). Reproduced: Welch, *Art of Mughal India: Painting and Precious Objects*, New York, 1963, p. 31, pl. 18; S.P. Verma, *Painting the Mughal Experience*, New Delhi, 2005, pp. 60-1, fig. 7 ("This portrait is undoubtedly superb in its rendering of the mood of the musician, delineating his physical features, and the stress on modelling and presentation of mass and volume").
15. Okada, op. cit., p. 92, fig. 95 ("Also typical of Basawan's style is the famous *The Dervish* in the Musee Guimet, the portrait of a real character the artist encountered one day in his path, rather than the stereotyped effigy of an Islamic mystic so typical of Persian and Mughal iconography."); Verma, op. cit., p. 61, fig. 8. Another drawing of roaming dervishes attributed to Basawan is described as rare: "Rare in other traditions, this type of portrait remained a fixure of Mughal art until the late seventeenth century" (Welch, op. cit., Cat. no. 9, p. 38). See also Pratapditya Pal, *Indian Painting*, Vol. I, California, 1993, Cat. no. 69, p. 257 ("Judging by the necklaces of beads, his crutch, and his attire, there seems little doubt that the man represents a holy personage. ... The face and the hands are superbly modelled, indicating that this is a sensitive study from life").
16. Okada, op. cit., p. 93, fig. 1 ("The holy man's face, deep in stern meditation, also displays the psychological insight typical of this great master."); Verma, op. cit., p. 61 ("The portrait of Jain ascetic, too, is unusual in that it is imbued with psychological insight").
17. T.W. Arnold and J.V.S. Wilkinson, *The Library of A. Chester Beatty: A Catalogue of the Indian Miniatures*, London, 1936, Vol. II, pls. 47-8. For the illustrations depicting yogic practices, see Vol. III, pl. 98. See also Okada, op. cit., p. 93 where she writes: "The illustrations of these two manuscripts yielded highly individualized portraits of holy men that amount to perceptive character studies."
18. Y.A. Godard, "Les marges du Murakka' Gulshan", *Athar-e Iran*, Vol. I, 1936, pp. 18-24, figs. 9, 10-4; Verma, op. cit., p. 128, no. 10, pls. XXVI-II, XXIX.
19. Reproduced and described: Milo C. Beach, *The Grand Mogul: Imperial Painting in India (1600-1660)*, Williamstown, Mass. 1978, p. 114, pl. on p. 114 (detail p. 115).
20. Jahangir, *Tuzuk-i Jahangiri* (1624), tr. A. Rogers, ed. H. Beveridge, London, 1904-14, Vol. II, pp. 116-17 ("At the time when I sent Khan Alam to Persia, I had sent with him a painter of the name of Bishan Das, who was unequalled in his age for taking likenesses, to take the portrait of the Shah and the chief men of his State, and bring them."). See also Verma, op. cit., pp. 110-11.
21. Welch, op. cit., p. 213, no. 140.
22. Published: 1. Stchoukine, *La Peinture Indienne a l'Epoque des Grands Moghols*, Paris, 1929, pl.44; see also Verma, op. cit., p. 106, no. 9, pl. XIV.
23. Welch, op. cit., pp. 242-43, no. 154.
24. Ibid., pp. 244-45.
25. For their reproduction, see S.C. Welch, *Art of Mughal India, & C.*, op. cit., p. 164, pl. 12; also in his *Imperial Mughal Painting*, New York, 1978, pp. 60, pl. 10 ("The villagers and their herds evoke today's India and must have been even more familiar to sixteenth-century viewer".); p. 70, pl. 16 (see the astrologers preparing prince's horoscope, seated against a red sandstone wall).
26. J. Marek, H. Knizkova and O. Kuthanova, *The Jenghis Khan Miniatures from the Court of Akbar the Great*, Czechoslovakia, 1963, p. 36. See also Shireen Moosvi, "Work and Gender in pre-colonial India" in Universita Boeeom, ed. *Socio-economic consequences of sex ratios in historical perspective, 1500-1900*, Milan, 1994, p. 105, where she writes that the well-known tradition of accuracy and realism seen in Mughal school makes its portrayals of scenes of the court and everyday life particularly significance for our purpose.
27. Ibid., p. 36, no. 5.
28. Ibid., p. 36, no. 29.
29. Ibid., p. 36, no. 11 and 16.

30. For the portraits of painters, see Godard, op. cit., pp. 18-22, figs. 9-14; Verma, *Mughal Painters and Their Work, & C.*, op. cit., pp. 105, 128, pls. XXVI-XLIX; Welch, *Art of Mughal India, & C.*, op. cit., pp. 31, 164-5, pl. 18.
31. For their reproduction, see Hamid Suleiman, *Miniatures of Baburnama*, Tashkent, 1970, pl. 27; M.S. Randhawa, *Paintings of the Baburnama*, New Delhi, 1983, p. 32, pl. VIII; S.J. Tyulayev, *Miniatures of Baburnamah*, Moscow, 1960, pl. 22; Welch, *Art of Mughal India & C.*, op. cit., pp. 27, 163, pl. 9. For a detailed description, see Verma, *Art and Material Culture in the Paintings of Akbar's Court*, New Delhi, 1978, pp. 19-20, pl. XVI.
32. See "Bookbinders at work" (*ca.* 1585-90), *Khamsa* of Nizami, Keir Collection Pontresina, V.34, f.184b (Reproduced and described: B.W. Robinson, ed., *Islamic Painting and the Arts of the Book, The Keir Collection*, London, 1976, pl. 117 (left). See also A.J. Qaisar and Rana Firdaus, "The Craft of Bookbinding in Mughal India"in A.J. Qaisar and S.P. Verma, eds. *Art and Culture, Endeavours in Interpretation*, New Delhi, 1996, pl. 26).
33. For reproduction, see Esin Atil, *The Brush of Masters: Drawings from Iran and India*, Washington, 1978, no. 63, pp. 106-7.
34. See "Textile workers" (*ca.* 1600), Johnson Album, India Office Library, London, V. 8, no. 5 (For a note on this illustration, see Verma "Sixteenth century miniatures at the Royal Library (Windsor) and India Office Library (London) – a survey of hitherto unnoticed paintings", *Proceedings of the Indian History Congress*, Bodh Gaya, 1981, pp. 263-64; also in his "Technology in Mughal India, Evidence of Mughal Painting" in A. Roy and S.K. Bagchi, eds. *Technology in Ancient and Medieval India*, Delhi, 1986, p. 20, pl. 13). See also Rana Firdaus, "A note on textile crafts depicted in Indian Painting", *Proceedings of Indian History Congress*, Kurukshetra, 1983, pp. 319-21). See also Robert Skelton, *The Indian Heritage, Court Life and Arts under Mughal Rule*, London, 1982, no. 23, p. 32.
35. See S.R. Sarma, "Scientific Instruments, Evidence from Mughal Painting" in A.J. Qaisar and S.P. Verma, eds. *Art and Culture, Painting and Perspective*, New Delhi, 2002, p. 87, pl. 86 (astrologer with his instruments); "An Arab and the baker" (*ca.* 1595-1600), *Anwar-i Suhaili*, Chester Beatty Library and Gallery of Oriental Art, Dublin (Reproduced: Linda Leach, op. cit., p. 160, fig. 228).
36. See folio 203 "Babur visiting camp" (*ca.* 1598-1600), *Baburnama*, National Museum (N.M. 50.326), New Delhi. (Reproduced: Rai Krishnadasa and Humyaun Kabir, *Mughal Miniatures*, New Delhi, 1955, pl. 2; Randhawa, op. cit., pp. 80, illustration p. 120).
37. Francois Bernier, *Travels in the Mughal Empire, 1656-68*, tr. A. Constable, reprint, New Delhi, 1968, p. 250.
38. See "Building of the fort at Agra", *Akbarnama* (*ca.* 1600-05), Victoria and Albert Museum, London, IS, 2-1896, no. 117, pl. 46 (Reproduced: Geeti Sen, op. cit., p. 87, pl. 32).
39. See "Building of Fathpur Sikri", *Akbarnama* (*ca.* 1600-05), Chester Beatty Library, Dublin, f.153 (Reproduced: T.W. Arnold and J.V.S. Wilkinson, *Library of Chester Beatty: A Catalogue of the Indian Miniatures*, London, 1936, Vol. II, pl. 24).
40. The miniature is lodged in the Prince of Wales Museum of Western India, Mumbai, Acc. No. 43.35. For reproduction, see Moti Chandra, *Indian Art*, Bombay, 1974, pl. XXXIII.
41. "An expedition scene: from Lahore to Akbarabad (Agra), *Padshahnama*, Royal Library, Windsor, No. 773, f.166b (*ca.* 1655). Reproduced and described: Verma, "Technology in Mughal India & C.", op. cit., p. 19, pl. 11.
42. See Verma, "Technology in Mughal India & C.", op. cit., p. 19, pl. 10 (A woman looking after the water-mill); Krishnadasa, op. cit., pp. 73, 76, pls. D and H; "Building of fort at Agra", "Akbar supervising building of Fathpur Sikri", *Akbarnama*, Victoria and Albert Museum, London, IS, 2-1896, no. 117, pls. 45-6, 86, 91 (Reproduced: Verma, *Art and Material Culture & C.*, op. cit., p. 117, pls. LXXVI-LXXVII; Sen, op. cit., pls. 31-2, 61); "Sultan Ghazan Khan builds "Gates of Piety" and charitable institutions in Tabriz", *Jami'-ut Tawarikh*, Gulistan Palace Museum, Teheran (Reproduced: Marek, Knizkova and Kuthanova, op. cit., p. 36, no. 29).

VILLAGE MEN AND WOMEN

1. Babur, *Baburnama* (1530), ed. and tr. A.S. Beveridge, London, 1921, p. 519. The *langota* [or *langoti*] is a kind of very narrow short *dhoti* worn in the same way and constituting the minimum of clothing (A.K. Coomaraswamy, *Catalogue of the Indian Collections in the Museum of Fine Arts, Boston*, Pt. V, Boston, 1926, p. 25).
2. Rai Krishnadasa, *Anwar-e-Suhaili (Iyar-i-Danish)*, Varanasi, 1999, pp. 73, 76, pls. D and H.
3. M.C. Beach, *The Imperial Image: Paintings for the Mughal Court*, Washington, D.C., 1981, p. 71, Cat. no. 6, illustration page 47; See also an illustration from *Mirgavat* (*ca.* 1525-70), published by Karl Khandalavala and Moti Chandra, *New Documents of Indian Painting: A Reappraisal*, Bombay, 1970, fig. 179.
4. For reproduction, see J.M. Rogers, *Mughal Miniatures*, London, 1993, figs. 25-6.
5. S.P. Verma, "Technology in Mughal India, Evidence of Mughal Painting" in A. Roy and S.K. Bagchi, eds. *Technology in Ancient and Medieval India*, Delhi, 1986, p. 19, pl. 11.
6. Folio from the *Mahapurana* (*ca.* 1540). Reproduced: Khandalavala and Chandra, op. cit., fig. 155 (a farm scene).
7. Moti Chandra, *Indian Art, Prince of Wales Museum of Western India*, Bombay, 1974, pl. XXXIII.
8. Geeti Sen, *Paintings from the Akbarnama*, New Delhi, 1984, pp. 87-91, pl. 32; B.W. Robinson, ed. *Islamic Painting and the Arts of the Book* (*The Keir Collection*), London, 1976, Cat. No.V.56, p. 123.
9. Peter Mundy, *Travels of Peter Mundy in Europe and Asia, 1608-67*, Vol. II, *Travels in Asia*, ed. R.C. Temple, London, 1914, pp. 110-11.
10. S.P. Verma, *Art and Material Culture in the Paintings of Akbar's Court*, New Delhi, 1978, p. 50 ("A wider variety of turbans, used by the commoners, were plain and simple [pl. XXXII, figs. 17-32]").
11. Verma, *Art and Material Culture* & C., op. cit., pp. 49-50, pl. XXXII.
12. Ibid., p. 51. See H. Knizkova, O. Kuthanova, and J. Marek, *The Jenghis Khan Miniatures from the Court of Akbar the Great*, Czechoslovakia, 1963, no.29; Geeti Sen, *Paintings from the Akbarnama*, New Delhi, 1984, pls. 31-2, 61; Rai Krishnadasa, op. cit., pls. D, H, and J.
13. Verma, op. cit., p. 115 ("Like the boatmen, the shepherds are shown dressed either scantily, in a loin cloth, or fully in short drawers, caps and even shoes – the latter rarely. The *jama* is shorter than that worn by the gentry .... When shown half-naked, there appears to be no difference between the shepherd and others of his class like the boatmen, fishermen and labourers"). See also p. 48 ("The *jama* of the commoners appears to be shorter—up to the knee or the middle of the thigh [pl. XXIX, figs. 4-5]"). See also F.R. Martin, *The Miniature Painting and Painters of Persia, India and Turkey*, London, 1912, Vol. II, pl. 180. M.C. Beach, *The Imperial Image: Paintings for the Mughal Court*, Washington, D.C. 1981, Cat. no. 3b, illustration page 40; J. Irwin, "The Heritage of Art in India: (3) the Mughal period", *Studio*, no. 135, 1948, illustration p. 41.
14. A. Rashid, *Society and Culture in Medieval India (1206-1556* AD*)*, Calcutta, p. 52.
15. K.M. Ashraf, *Life and Conditions of the People of Hindustan*, New Delhi, 1970, p. 124.
16. See Verma, op. cit., pls. LXXVI-LXXVII; Sen, op. cit., pls. 31-2, detail, pls. 30, 33.
17. See Knizkova, *et al.*, op. cit., no.29.
18. Jean-Baptiste Tavernier, *Travels in India, 1640-67*, tr. V. Ball, ed. William, Crooke, reprint, Delhi, 1977, Vol. II, pp. 59-60.
19. For *peshwaz*, see Abu'l Fazl, *A'in-i Akbari* (1595), tr. H. Blochmann, Vol. I, Calcutta, 1965, p. 94 ("The *peshwaz* (a coat open in front) is of the same form, but tied in front. It is sometimes made without strings"); Verma, op. cit., p. 49, pl. XXX, fig. 3.
20. *Baburnama*, op. cit., p. 519.
21. Verma, op. cit., pls. LXXVI-LXXVII.
22. Toby Falk, Simon Digby, and Michael Goedhuis, *Painting from Mughal India*, London, n.d., p. 56.
23. Robert Sketton, "Mughal Paintings from Harivamsa Manuscript", *Victoria and Albert Museum Year Book*, No. 2, London, 1970, illustration p. 42.
24. L. Binyon and T.W. Arnold, *The Court Painters of the Grand Moguls*, London, 1921, pl.XVIII; J. Irvin, "The Heritage of Art in India: III The Mughal Period", *Studio*, Vol. CXXXV, no. 659, 1948, illustration p. 41. A.K. Coomaraswamy, "Notes on Indian Painting, Bishandas and others", *Artibus Asiae*, No. 4, MCMXXVII, Hellerau-Dresden, fig. 22; Falk, *et al.*, op. cit., p. 56, pl. 26.

25. Thomas Roe and John Fryer, *Travels in India in the Seventeenth Century*, Reprint, New Delhi, 1993, p. 454.
26. M.S. Randhawa, *Paintings of the Baburnama*, New Delhi, 1983, pl. on page 109.
27. A. Jan Qaisar, "*The Miftah-ul Fuzala*: A Study of an Illustrated Persian Lexicon" in A. Jan Qaisar and S.P. Verma, eds. *Art and Culture: Painting and Perspective*, New Delhi, 2002, p. 27, fig. 12.
28. S.P. Verma, "Technology in Mughal India, Evidence of Mughal Painting" in A. Roy and S.K. Bagchi, eds. *Technology in Ancient and Medieval India*, Delhi, 1986, p. 19, pl. 10.
29. See Ishrat Alam, "Textile Tools as depicted in Ajanta and Mughal Painting" in Roy and Bagchi, op. cit., pp. 129-30, pl. 29.
30. I.B. Horner, "Women under Primitive Buddhism: Laywomen and Alms women" in Kumkum Roy, ed. *Women in Early Indian Societies*, New Delhi, 1999, p. 87.
31. Verma, "Technology in Mughal India, Evidence of Mughal Painting", op. cit., p. 16, pl. 1; Ishrat Alam, op. cit., p. 132, pl. 34. See also Qaisar, op. cit., p. 24, fig. 4.
32. For reproduction, see S.C. Welch, *Imperial Mughal Painting*, New York, 1978, p. 60, pl. 10.
33. For their reproduction, see S.P. Verma, *Mughal Painters and Their Work: A Biographical Survey and Descriptive Catalogue*, New Delhi, 1994, p. 106, pl. XIV; F.R. Martin, *The Miniature Painting and Painters of Persia, India and Turkey*, London, 1912, Vol. II, pl. 207 A (A warrior conversing with a saint). See Irfan Habib, *The Agrarian System of Mughal India (1556-1607)*, Delhi, 1963, p. 58; Rekha Misra, *Women in Mughal India (1526-1748* AD), Delhi, 1967, p. 130.
34. See R.P. Srivastava, *Punjab Painting*, New Delhi, 1983, fig. 104 (Weaver and Bhago weaveress).
35. M.S. Randhawa, *Kangra Painting of the Bhagavata Purana*, New Delhi, 1960, p. 50, pl. V.
36. S.P. Verma, *Indian at Work in Sculpture and Painting*, Aligarh, 1994, pl. VI, Rai Krishnadasa, *Anwar-e-Suhaili (Iyar-i-Danish)*, Varanasi, 1999, pp. 77-8, pl. I ("The depiction of the washing couple throws light about a particular event of daily life in the sixteenth century. It is notably significant that in court painting, normal social life has hardly been found depicted").
37. "Washerman at home" (*ca.* 1600), *Razmnama*, British Museum, London, Or.12076, f.48a. Published: Verma, *India at Work & C.*, op. cit., pl. XX.
38. See G.L. Possehl, *The Indus Civilization: A Contemporary Perspective*, New Delhi, 2002, p. 182, fig. 10.10.
39. Women engaged in household work: husking rice in mortar, crushing grain with stone pestle, winnowing rice, and rolling dough for cake. Detail from Sanchi Stupa no.1, *ca.*50 BC to AD 100 Published: Verma, *India at Work & C.*, op. cit., pl. III.
40. "Yashoda churning butter". Detail from Lingaraja Temple (AD 1000), Bubaneshwar, Orissa. Published: Verma, *India at Work & C.*, op. cit., pl. IV.
41. Randhawa, *Kangra Painting & C.*, op. cit., p. 46, pl. III; Kandalavala and Chandra, op. cit., fig. 144.
42. Vijya Ramaswamy, "Aspects of Women at Work in Early South India" in Kumkum Roy, op. cit., p. 166.
43. Romila Thapar, *Asoka and the Decline of the Mauryas*, New Delhi, 1961, p. 86.
44. Rashid, op. cit., p. 143.
45. Sylvia Crowe and Sheila Haywood, *The Gardens of Mughal India*, Delhi, 1973, pl. on p. 39 (see woman as a agricultural labourer).
46. Shireen Moosvi, "Society, Part II, India", *History of Civilization of Central Asia*, Vol. V, eds. Chahryar Adle and Irfan Habib, Co-editor, Karl M. Baipakoo, Paris, 2003, p. 368 and n. 146.
47. "Women husking rice". Damodar Temple at Kalyanpur, Howrah (West Bengal), *ca.*AD 1786. Published: Verma, *India at Work & C.*, op. cit., pl. XXIV.
48. See Possehl, op. cit., p. 182, fig. 10.9.
49. "Women seller" (*ca.* 1720), Pahari School (Mankot), Prince of Wales Museum of Western India, Mumbai (Published: Linda Leach, "Life at Court" in *Image of Man: The Indian Perception of the Universe through 2000 years of Painting and Sculpture*, Delhi, 1982, p. 160, fig. 227; "Women sellers" (Company School) in Mildred Archer, *Company Paintings, Indian Paintings of the British Period*, London, 1992, Cat. no. 58, pp. 90-1.
50. Tavernier, op. cit., Vol. I, p. 45.
51. For the reproduction, see Arnold and Wilkinson, op. cit., Vol. I, p. 9, Vol. II, pl. 24.
52. Tavernier, op. cit., Vol. II, p. 59.
53. Ibid., p. 60.

54. M. de Thevenot, *Indian Travels of Thevenot and Careri*, ed. S. Sen, New Delhi, 1949, pp. 55-56.
55. Ishrat Alam, "Diamond Mining and Trade in South India in the Seventeenth Century", *The Medieval History Journal*, New Delhi, 3, 2 (2000), pp. 299, 301.

WORKMEN AND PROFESSIONALS

1. See S.P. Verma, *Art and Material Culture in the Paintings of Akbar's Court*, New Delhi, 1978, p. 116 ("The masons are seen with a turban, a short *jama*, and short trousers. They often wear shoes, which, for their variety among the workmen, may be taken as a mark of respectability"), pls. LXXVI-LXXVII; L. Binyon and T.W. Arnold, *The Court Painters of the Grand Moguls*, London, 1921, p. 70, pl. VIII; J. Marek, H. Knizkova and O. Kuthanova, *The Jenghiz Khan Miniatures from the Court of Akbar the Great*, Czechoslovakia, 1963, no. 29; Robert Skelton, *The Indian Heritage, Court Life and Arts under Mughal Rule*, London, 1982, p. 34, no. 30 (Akbar inspecting the building of the new city of Fathpur Sikri).
2. Abu'l Fazl, *Ain-i Akbari* (1595), tr. H. Blochmann, Vol. I, Calcutta, 1965, pp. 235-36.
3. Irfan Habib, "Exploring Medieval Gender History", *Symposia Papers: 23*, Calicut, 2000, p. 3.
4. F. Pelsaert, *The Remonstrantie (Jahangir's India)*, tr. W.H. Moreland, and P. Geyl, Delhi, 1972, p. 60.
5. Jean-Baptiste Tavernier, *Travels in India, 1640-67*, tr. V. Ball, ed. William Crooke, reprint, Delhi, 1977, Vol. II, p. 46.
6. Ishrat Alam, "Diamond Mining and Trade in South India in the Seventeenth Century", *The Medieval History Journal*, New Delhi, 3, 2 (2000), p. 302.
7. De Laet Joannes, *Empire of the Great Mogol*, tr. J.S. Hoyland, annotated by S.N. Banerjee, Bombay, 1928, pp. 88-9.
8. Ibid., pp. 94-5.
9. Francois Bernier, *Travels in the Mogul Empire, AD 1656-68*, tr. A. Constable, revised V.A. Smith, First Indian Edition, New Delhi, 1983, p. 205.
10. Ibid., pp. 254-55.
11. Ibid., p. 227.
12. Ibid., p. 225.
13. Alexander I. Tchitcherov, *India, Changing Economic Structure in the Sixteenth-Eighteenth Centuries, Outline History of Crafts and Trade*, New Delhi, 1998, p. 161.
14. Irfan Habib, *The Agrarian System of Mughal India*, Delhi, 1963, pp. 150, 239, 248.
15. M.S. Commissariat, *Mandelslo's Travels in Western India* (AD *1638-9)*, Bombay, 1931, p. 9.
16. Mohammad Yasin, *A Social History of Islamic India, 1605-1748*, Lucknow, 1958, p. 28.
17. Ibid., p. 29.
18. Ibid., p. 29.
19. A bazaar scene, *ca.* 1600. Folio from the *Anwar-i Suhaili*, Chester Beatty Library, Dublin. Published: Linda Leach, "Life and Court" in *The Image of Man: The Indian Perspective of the Universe through 2000 years of Painting and Sculpture*, Delhi, 1982, fig. 228. It is notable that in ancient times pedlars and hawkers sold their trumpery and trinkets from door to door (Jeannine Auboyer, *Daily life in Ancient India*, London, 1965, p. 121).
20. Bernier, op. cit., p. 250.
21. Ibid.
22. Thomas Roe and John Fryer, *Travels in India in the Seventeenth Century*, London, 1873, p. 454.
23. Ibid.
24. Reproduced: S.R. Sarma, "Scientific Instruments, Evidence from Mughal Painting" in A.J. Qaisar and S.P. Verma, eds. *Art and Culture, Painting and Perspective*, New Delhi, 2002, p. 87, pl. 86.
25. Bernier, op. cit., pp. 243-44.
26. For reproduction, see Pratapaditya Pal and others, *Romance of the Taj Mahal*, New Delhi, 1989, p. 116, fig. 116.
27. For reproduction, see Lubor Hajek, *Indian Miniatures From the Mughal School*, London, 1960, p. 86, pl. 18; See also A.S. Melikian-Chiravani, "Mir Sayeed 'Ali: Painter of the Past and Pioneer of the Future" in A.K. Das, ed. *Mughal Masters: Further Studies*, Mumbai, 1998, p. 38. fig. 7 (an astrologer holding a ring-

dial). For the description of ring-dial, sandglass, etc., see Verma, *Art and Material Culture & C.*, op. cit., pp. 112-13, pl. LXVIII, figs. 55-6, Sarma, op. cit., pp. 85-6, 88-90, pl. 83-5.

28. A. Rashid, *Society and Culture in Medieval India* (1206-1556 AD), Calcutta, 1969, p. 83.
29. Rekha Misra, *Women in Mughal India*, New Delhi, 1967, pp. 82-3.
30. John Campbell Oman, *Cults, Customs and Superstitions of India*, Delhi, 1972, p. 238.
31. Ibid., p. 215. See also "Visit to a *faqir* by women accompanied with child", Bikaner School, *ca.* 1700. Published: Vishakha N. Desai, "Portraits, Hunts, Harems and Darbars, The Courtly Paintings of Rajasthan", *Orientations*, Hongkong, 1985, p. 39, fig. 6.

HOLY MEN

1. L. Bonyon and T.W. Arnold, *The Court Painters of the Grand Moguls*, London, 1921, pp. 57-8, 61, pls. XVIII and XXVIII; M.C. Beach, *The Imperial Image: Paintings for the Mughal Court*, Washington, D.C. 1981, Cat. no. 29, illustration p. 201; also in his *The New Cambridge History of India: Mughal and Rajput Painting*, Cambridge, 1992, figs. 59-60; and "The Mughal painter Daswanth", *Arts Orientalis*, Michigan, Vol. 13, 1982, p. 124, fig. 10-11; Robert Skelton, *L'Inde des Legendes et des Realities, Miniatures Indiennes et Persanes*, Paris, no date, no. 12, p. 11, pl. 10 and no. 13, p. 12, pl. 11; J.V.S. Wilkinson, "A note on an illustrated manuscript of *Jog-Bashisht*", *Bulletin of the School of Oriental Studies*, London, No. 12, 1968, pls. 6-8, 10; S.C. Welch, *Indian Drawings and Painted Sketches, 16th through 19th Centuries*, New York, 1976, Cat. no. 9 (dervishes), p. 38; no. 19, pp. 50-1; B.W. Robinson, ed., *Islamic Painting and the Arts of the Book* (*The Keir Collection*), London, 1976, Cat. no. V. 56, pl. 123; V. 68, pl. 125; A.A. Ivanova, *et al.*, *Al'bom Indiyskikh-I Pyersidskikh Miniatyar XVI-XVIIIvv*, Moscow, 1962, pp. 77, 79, pls. 12-3, 68 (left); Hamid Suleiman, *Miniatures of Babur-nama*, Tashkent, 1970, pls. 29, 54; A.K. Srivastava, *Mughal Painting, an Interplay of Indigenous and Foreign Traditions*, New Delhi, 2000, pls. Nos. III. 24 (encampment of dervishes) and III.56.
   They look alike the holy men of ancient India. Jeannine Auboyer observes that *sadhus* (religious mendicants) were also to be seen, almost naked, and their bodies smeared with ashes (*Daily Life in Ancient India*, London, 1961, p. 122 see also fig. 11).
2. See William Foster, *Early Travels in India, 1583-1619*, First Indian Edition, New Delhi, 1981, pp. 19-20.
3. Ibid., p. 319.
4. Francois Bernier, *Travels in the Mogul Empire, AD 1656-68*, tr. A. Constable, revised V.A. Smith, First Indian Edition, New Delhi, 1983, pp. 316-17.
5. Jean-Baptiste Tavernier, *Travels in India*, tr. V.Ball, First Indian Edition, New Delhi, 1977, Vol. I, p. 67.
6. Beach, *Mughal and Rajput Painting*, op. cit., pl. 60 (notice the holy man blessing the child); Pramod Chandra, "Ustad Salivahana and the development of Popular Mughal Art", *Lalit Kala*, No. 8, New Delhi, 1960, fig. 36 (hermit blessing a child).
7. See M.C. Beach, *The Imperial Image: Paintings for the Mughal Court*, Washington, D.C., 1981, Cat. no. 30 (Sultan Parviz with an ascetic), illustration p. 202; Beach, *Mughal and Rajput Painting*, op. cit., pl. 110 (Dara and a holyman); Y.A. Godard, "Un album de portraits des princes Timurides de l'Inde", *Athar-e Iran*, Vol. II, 1937, Cat. no. 11, fig. 69, no. 13, fig. 71, and no. 43, fig. 93. Biyon and Arnold, op. cit., pls. VI and XVII; Robinson, op. cit., Cat. no. 95, pl. 134; S.C. Welch, "Mughal and Deccani Miniature Paintings from a Private Collection", *Arts Orientalis*, Vol. 5, Michigan, 1963, Cat. no. 4, fig. 5; R. Ettinghausen, "The Emperor's choice", *De Artibus Opuscula*, XL, New York, 1961, p. 33, figs. 13-4.
8. Babur, *Baburnama* (1530), ed. and tr. A.S. Beveridge, London, 1921, p. 230. See also p. 394.
9. For reproduction, see Hamid Suleiman, *Miniatures of Babur-nama*, Tashkent, 1970, pl. 29.
10. For other illustrations of *kanphata* yogis, see Toby Falk and Mildred Archer, *Indian Miniatures in the India Office Library*, London, 1981, Cat. Nos. 25 and 145, illustration pp. 356, 366, 418.
11. Walter Smith, "Hindu Ascetics in Mughal Painting under Akbar", *Oriental Art*, New Series, Vol. 27, No. 1, London, 1981, p. 73, figs. 9-10.
12. See Pratapaditya Pal and Others, *Romance of the Taj Mahal*, New Delhi, 1989, pl. 110.
13. Bernier, op. cit., p. 317.
14. Saiyid Athar Abbas Rizvi, *A History of Sufism in India*, Vol. I, Delhi, 1983, p. 369.

15. S.P. Verma, "Similar Themes, Different Treatment: The Mughal Experience" in A.J. Qaisar and S.P. Verma, eds. *Art and Culture: Painting and Perspective*, New Delhi, 2002, p. 64, pls. 59-61.
16. See Abu'l Fazl, *Ain-i Akbari* (1595), tr. H. Blochmann, Vol. I, Calcutta, 1965, p. 117, pl. XII, fig. 25. It was not a weapon of the Mughal soldier, though Abu'l Fazl has mentioned it. S.P. Verma, *Art and Material Culture in the Paintings of Akbar's Court*, New Delhi, 1978, p. 95, pl. LXII, fig. 26 ("The *chakra* (quoit) ... was a flat metallic ring with a sharp razor-like outer edge. *Sannyasis* and *jogis* wielded it.").
17. For a description of this instrument, see *A'in-i Akabri*, op. cit., Vol. III, tr., Jarrett, Calcutta, 1894, p. 269; Verma, *Art and Material Culture & C.*, op. cit., p. 69, pl. LIII, figs. 7-8. See also p. 80 (the *morchal*, made from peacock feathers, became more popular toward the later phase of the sixteenth century).
18. Smith, op. cit., p. 69. For the reproduction of the miniature, see Suleiman, op. cit., pl. 29.
19. Arnold and Wilkinson, op. cit., Vol. II, pls. 48-9.
20. Smith, op. cit., pp. 72-3, fig. 6; John Campbell Oman, *The Mystics, Ascetics and Saints*, London, 1905, p. 43.
21. Smith, op. cit., pp. 72-3; Oman, op. cit., p. 39, where he writes that the life-like portrait of hermit identical in two illustrations is in all probability a living model of the age.
22. Amina Okada, "Basawan" in Pratapaditya Pal, ed. *Master Artists of the Imperial Mughal Court*, Mumbai, 1991, p. 13, fig. 15.
23. Ibid. In an anonymous work, datable 1585-90, an ascetic is also shown accompanied with a dog (Okada, op. cit., p. 13, fig. 14). See also Beach, *Mughal and Rajput Painting*, op. cit., pls. 59-60 (note ascetics accompanied with a dog). Welch, op. cit., p. 38, no. 9. See also S.C. Welch, "Mughal and Deccani Miniature Paintings from a Private Collection", *Ars Orientalis*, Vol. 5, Michigan, 1963, Cat. no. 7, fig. 6 (a dervish with a long horn suspended from a cord around his neck).
24. S.P. Verma, *Painting the Mughal Experience*, New Delhi, 2005, p. 61, fig. 8.
25. Robinson, op. cit., Cat. no. V.56, pl. 123; Hamid Suleiman, *Miniatures of the Babur-nama*, Tashkent, 1970, pl. 54.
26. Rizvi, op. cit., Vol. II, p. 107.
27. Y.A. Godard, "Un album de portraits des princes Timurides de l'Inde", *Athar-e Iran*, Vol. II, 1937, Cat. no. 14, pp. 200-04, figs. 71-2; Binyon and Arnold, op. cit., pp. 85-6, pl. XXXIII; Falk and Archer, op. cit., Cat. no. 96(ii), illustration p. 406. See Pratapaditya Pal, *Indian Painting*, Vol. I, California, 1993, Cat. no. 88, p. 299; Daniel J. Ehnbom, ed. *Indian Miniatures: The Ehrenfeld Collection*, New York, 1985, Cat. no. 16; Robinson, op. cit., Cat. no. V.102, pl. 137.
28. Jahangir, *Tuzuk-i Jahangiri* (1624), tr. A. Rogers, ed. H. Bveridge, London, 1904-14, Vol. II, p. 119.
29. For reproduction, see D. Barrett and B. Gray, *Painting of India*, Lausanne, 1963, pp. 99-100, illustration page 101 ("Undoubtedly the most remarkable of the miniatures in this little book is the *Dervishes dancing*. The abandon with which the two elderly dervishes are turning is implied by their turbans fallen to the ground. A third old man sings as he plays on the guitar to the accompaniment of a tambourine. Behind, a bearded man has flung his arms around the shoulders of a youth seated close beside him. The atmosphere of ecstasy is so strong that one is not surprised to see blue cherubs gazing down from the clouds above them."). For a painting of dervishes dancing before the court and ladies (British Museum, London (Stowe, Or. 16). See also M.C. Beach, *The Grand Mogul: Imperial Painting in India, 1600-1660*, Williamstown, 1978, p. 66, fig. 17 (a youth's ecstatic trance).
30. See T.W. Arnold and L. Binyon, *The Court Painters of the Grand Moguls*, Oxford, 1921, p. 61, pl. XVIII; Ivanova, *et al.*, op. cit., p. 78, pl. 42.
31. A. Rashid, *Society and Culture in Medieval India (1206-1556 AD)*, Calcutta, 1969, p. 209.
32. Thomas Roe and John Fryer, *Travels in India in the Seventeenth Century*, Reprint, New Delhi, 1993, pp. 450-51.

FOOD AND USE OF TOBACCO

1. A. Rashid, *Society and Culture in Medieval India (1206-1556 AD)*, Calcutta, 1969, p. 47 (boiled rice mixed with pulse).
2. Abu'l Fazl, *Ain-i Akbari* (1595), tr. H.S. Jarrett, Calcutta, 1894, Vol. II, p. 240.
3. Jahangir, *Tuzuk-i Jahangiri* (1624), tr. A. Rogers, ed. H. Beveridge, London, 1904-14, Vol. I, p. 419.

4. Françisco Pelsaert, *"Remonstrantie"* (1626), tr. W. Moreland, and Geyl, *Jahangir's India*, Cambridge, 1925, Reprint, Delhi, 1972, p. 60.
5. Francois Bernier, *Travels in Mughal India,* AD *1656-1668,* tr. A. Constable, revised, V.A. Smith, First Indian Edition, New Delhi, 1983, p. 152.
6. Jean Baptiste Tavernier, *Travels in India*, tr. V. Ball, First Indian Edition, New Delhi, 1977, Vol. I, p. 311. Also see p. 225 (*khichri* – a dish of boiled rice and *dal*, a kind of pulse (*Cajanus indicus*).
7. Ibid.
8. Thomas Roe and John Fryer, *Travels in India in the Seventeenth Century,* Reprint, New Delhi, 1993, pp. 454-55.
9. Pelsaert, op. cit., p. 48, where it is further mentioned that the cakes of the cow-dung were also sold as peat in Holland.
10. Ibid., p. 61.
11. De Laet Joannes, *Empire of the Great Mogol*, tr. J.S. Hoyland, annotated by S.N. Banerjee, Bombay, 1928, p. 90.
12. Bernier, op. cit., p. 368.
13. See Susan Stronge, *Painting for the Mughal Emperor: The Art of the Book 1560-1660,* Delhi, 2002, p. 26, illustration on page 17 (folio from *Hamzanama, ca.* 1570); also p. 159, pl. 122 (a singer and companion, *ca.* 1640); R. Skelton, "Mughal Paintings from the Harivamsa, Manuscript", Victoria and Albert Museum Year Book, No. 2, London, 1970, illustration p. 42 (note earthen pitchers); De Laet Joannes, op. cit., p. 89 (earthen vessels).
14. Skelton, op. cit., illustration p. 42 (churning of butter).
15. See S.P. Verma, *Art and Material Culture in the Paintings of Akbar's Court,* New Delhi, 1978, p. 55, pl. XXXVI, fig. 7 ("The *lota* used by masons or labourers is rarely represented .... It is an earthen pot with a small body, flat bottom, small neck, opening out broadly like a funnel and a small spout for pouring the water. This type of *lota* is known nowadays as *badhna*").
16. *Tuzuk-i Jahangiri,* op. cit., Vol. I, p. 357. John Hvighen van Linschoten in Samuel Purchas, *Purchas: His Pilgrimes,* Vol. X, London, MCMV, p. 248. See also A. Rashid, *Society and Culture in Medieval India (1206-1556* AD*),* Calcutta, 1969, p. 59.
17. Samuel Purchas, *Purchas: His Pilgrimes,* Vol. X, Glasgow, MCMV, p. 248 ("They use to drinke out of a Copper kanne with a spout, whereby they let the water fall downe into their mouthes, and never touch the Pot with their lippes.")
18. Babur, *Baburnama* (1530), ed. and tr. A.S., Beveridge, London, 1921, pp. 518-19.
19. A.A. Ivanova, *et al., Albom Indiyskikh-i Pyersidskikh Miniatyar XVI-XVIIIvv,* Moscow, 1962, p. 80, pl. 76.
20. K.M. Ashraf, *Life and Conditions of the People of Hindustan,* New Delhi, 1970, p. 264. See miniatures, "Prince with his companions" (*ca.* 1625), Victoria and Albert Museum, IS, 9-1965 (L. Asthon, ed., *The Art of India and Pakistan,* London, 1948, p. 166, no. 758, pl. 11); "Zafar Khan with poets and scholars", *Masnavi* of Zafar Khan (dated 1663), Royal Asiatic Society, London, MS Persian 310 (J.P. Losty, *The Art of the Book,* London, 1982, no. 83, fig. on p. 100); "Princesses with attendants", Freer Gallery of Art, Washington, no. 07, 213 (Esin Atil, *The Brush of the Masters: Drawing from Iran and India,* Washington, 1978, p. 120, no. 73). It corroborates Irfan Habib's assertion that by Shah Jahan's reign tobacco had found a place in the perfumery of aristocratic households [*The Agrarian System of Mughal India (1556-1707*), Delhi, 1963, p. 45].
21. See miniature "Sages conversing" (*ca.* 1650), Hermitage, Leningrad (A.A. Ivanova, *et al., Albom Indiyskikh-i Pyersidskikh Miniatyar XV-XVIIvv,* Moscow, 1962, pl. 40. See also pls. 68, 72 and 91. Here, it is noteworthy that tobacco smoking is absent in case of the commoners, in general. But see Habib, op. cit., p. 94 where he observes that by the end of Aurangzeb's reign (1707), tobacco smoking had already become a mass habit. See further A. Jan Qaisar, *Indian Response to European Technology and Culture (*AD *1498-1707*), New Delhi, 1982, pp. 120-22.
22. Fry Sebastien Manrique, *Travels of Fray Sebastien Manrique 1629-1643* by C.K. Eckford Luard, Oxford, 1927, Vol. II, p. 250 & n. 4. See also William Foster, *Early Travels in India, 1583-1619,* First Indian Edition, New Delhi, 1981, p. 299, where Edward Terry (1616-1619) observes that in Gujarat they sowe tobacco in abundance, but know not how to cure and make it strong, as those in the Western India [i.e., the West

Indies]; W.H. Moreland, *India at the Death of Akbar*, Delhi, 1920, p. 158, where he writes that tobacco plant was first established in the province of Gujarat where the leaf was obtainable in 1613.

23. *Tuzuk-i Jahangiri*, op. cit., Vol. I, p. 370. Here Jahangir further writes: "My brother Shah Abbas had also become aware of the mischief of arising from it, and had ordered that in Iran no one should venture to smoke."
24. M. de Thevenot, *Indian Travels of Thevenot and Careri*, ed. S. Sen, New Delhi, 1949, p. 280.
25. *Tuzuk-i Jahangiri*, Vol. I, p. 371.
26. M.S. Commissariat, *Mandelslo's Travels in Western India* (AD *1638-9)*, Bombay, 1931, p. 34.
27. Roe and Fryer, op. cit., pp. 454-55.
28. Tavernier, op. cit., Vol. I, p. 225.
29. Niccolao Manucci, *Storia do Mogor, 1656-1712*, tr. W. Irvine, London, 1907-08, Vol. II, p. 175 ("The Mahomedans consume a great deal of this article of smoking").
30. Manucci, op. cit., Vol. II, p. 175.

DWELLINGS AND HUT-SETTLEMENTS

1. S.C. Welch, *India, Art and Culture, 1300-1900*, New York, 1985, Cat. no. 93a, illustration p. 156, Cat. no. 159, illustration p. 243, Cat. no. 160, illustration p. 244; Susan Stronge, *Painting for the Mughal Emperor: The Art of the Book, 1560-1660*, New Delhi, 2002, pl. 122.
2. Babur, *Baburnama* (1530), ed. and tr. A.S. Beveridge, London, 1921, pp. 467-68.
3. See William Foster, *Early Travels in India, 1583-1619*, First Indian Edition, New Delhi, 1981, pp. 23-4. See also Samuel Purchas, *Purchas: His Pilgrimes*, Vol. X, London, MCMV, p. 180 ('The houses are simple, made of earth and covered with straw'), and p. 262, where John Hvighen van Linchoten during his voyage to Goa, in 1583, observes that the country men tilling the land and fishing, etc., lived very poorly: "They lived in little straw Houses, the doors where of are so low, that men must creepe in it and out, theire household stuffe is a Mat upon the ground to sleepe upon, and a Pit or hole in the ground to beat their Rice in, with a Pot or two to seeth it in, and so they live and gaine so much as it is a wonder".
4. Françisco Pelsaert, "*Remonstrantie*" (1626), tr. W. Moreland, and Geyl, *Jahangir's India*, Cambridge, 1925, Reprint, Delhi, 1972, p. 61.
5. Thomas Roe and John Fryer, *Travels in India in the Seventeenth Century*, Reprint, New Delhi, 1993, p. 455.
6. Pietro delle Valle (1623), *The Travels of Pietro delle Valle in India*, ed. Gray Edward, and tr. G. Havers, London, Vol. II, 1892, p. 360.
7. Jean Baptiste Tavernier, *Travels in India*, tr. V. Ball, First Indian Edition, New Delhi, 1977, Vol. I, p. 100. See also De Laet Joannes, *Empire of the Great Mogol*, tr. J.S. Hoyland, annotated by S.N. Banerjee, Bombay, 1928, p. 77 ("Patenaw is a large town, oblong in space: in the neighbourhood there are said to be many gold mines: the houses are of moderate size, mostly built of mud and thatched: but the streets are quite wide").
8. Tavernier, op. cit., Vol. I, p. 105.
9. Ibid., p. 6. See also p. 42 ("... the houses of which are for the most part thatched [at Burhanpur]".
10. Francois Bernier, *Travels in Mughal India*, AD *1656-1668*, tr. A. Constable, revised, V.A. Smith, First Indian Edition, New Delhi, 1983, pp. 246-47.
11. Foster, op. cit., p. 301; Purchas, op. cit., p. 248 ("Their Houses are commonly strawed with Kow-dung, which (they say) killeth Fleas"); Roe and Fryer, op. cit., p. 455("[Houses of poormen are] floored with cow-dung which they do afresh everyday, after they have swept and cleansed them. ...They plaster cow-dung before their doors, and so keep them clean, ...").
12. Niccolao Manucci, *Storia do Mogor, 1656-1712*, tr. W. Irvine, London, 1907-08, Vol. III, p. 41.
13. Edward Farley Oaten, *European Travellers in India*, Lucknow, 1974, p. 68 ("They worship a cow", he says, "and esteem much of the cow's dung to paint the walls of their houses...").
14. De Laet Joannes, *Empire of the Great Mogol*, tr. J.S. Hoyland, annotated by S.N. Banerjee, Second Edition, New Delhi, 1974, p. 81.
15. M. De Thevenot, *Indian Travels of Thevenot and Careri*, ed. S. Sen, New Delhi, 1949, p. 246.
16. M.S. Commissariat, *Mandelslo's Travels in Western India* (AD *1638-9)*, Bombay, 1931, p. 29.
17. Tavernier, op. cit., Vol. I, p. 233.

TRAVELLING

1. Abu'l Fazl, *A'in-i Akbari* (1595), tr. H. Blochmann, Vol. I, Calcutta, 1868, p. 159.
2. See William Foster, *Early Travels in India, 1583-1619*, New Delhi, First Indian Edition, 1981, p. 311 ("as fast as a horse").
3. Peter Mundy, *The Travels of Peter Mundy in Europe and Asia*, ed. R.C. Temple, Vol. II, p. 192, illustration no. 12.
4. Ibid.
5. Jean Baptiste Tavernier, *Travels in India*, tr. V. Ball, First Indian Edition, New Delhi, 1977, Vol. II, p. 190; M. de Thevenot, *Indian Travels of Thevenot and Careri*, ed. S. Sen, New Delhi, 1949, p. 263. See also Khursheed Mustafa, "Travels in Mughal India", *Medieval India Quarterly*, Vol. III, nos. 3 & 4, New Delhi, 1958, p. 270 ("Horse, elephants, camels, bullocks, bullock-carts of several designs and litters and palkeys of various types were the common means of travel, heavy luggage was transported by camels or bullocks, while the very poor travelled on foot and carried their loads themselves"); Abul Khair Muhammad Farooque, *Roads and Communications in Mughal India*, Delhi, 1977, p. 84. Subhash Parihar, *Land Transport in Mughal India: Agra-Lahore Mughal Highway and its Architectural Remains*, New Delhi, 2008, pp. 14-5.
6. Tavernier, op. cit., pp. 35-6.
7. Ibid., p. 36.
8. M. de Thevenot, *Indian Travels of Thevenot and Careri*, ed. S. Sen, New Delhi, 1949, p. 73.
9. J. Ovington, *A Voyage in Surat in the year 1689*, London, 1929, p. 254.
10. Farooque, op. cit., p. 105. See also Milo C. Beach, *The New Cambridge History of India: Mughal and Rajput Painting*, Cambridge, 1992, fig. 46.
11. See S.P. Verma, *Art and Material Culture in the Paintings of Akbar's Court*, New Delhi, 1978, p. 107, pl. LXX, fig. 1 ("Carriages were used both for travelling and carrying loads, the standard type of which seems to have been employed by the common people. Its main seat was sometimes built with side supports"). For the illustration of bullock cart used by the ordinary men, see Verma, op. cit., pl. LXXVI.
12. De Laet Joannes, *Empire of the Great Mogol*, tr. J.S. Hoyland, annotated by S.N. Banerjee, Second Edition, New Delhi, 1974, p. 83.
13. See *Akbarnama*, Victoria and Albert Museum, London, IS, 2-1896, no. 117, pl. 46 (Reproduced: Verma, op. cit., pl. LXXVII).
14. *A'in-i Akbari*, op. cit., Vol. I, p. 152.
15. Ibid., p. 160.
16. See M.S. Randhawa, *Paintings of the Baburnama*, New Delhi, 1983, illustration p. 119 (f. 194).
17. Edward Gray, *The Travels of Pietro della Valle in India*, Vol. I, London, MDCCXCII, p. 21.
18. Ibid., p. 65.
19. Ibid., pp. 65-6. See also pp. 118-19, where he writes: "We pass'd over the five *Cos* of wet ground with the four Currents of Water, of which the second was the deepest (having waited a while for a fit hour), in company of a numerous *Cafila* of Coaches, Cars, Horse-men and Footmen in the same manner and circumstances as I writ before; only the water was now much higher than we had found it at our Coming, so that it came into all the Coaches, and we were fain to stand upright and hold fast by the roof of the Coaches, bare leg'd too, because the water came above the bottom of the Coaches to the middle of the leg. The Oxen and Horses could scarce keep their Heads above Water, and the Coaches being light, if men hir'd purposely had not gone along in the water to hold them stready, and break the course thereof by holding great Stumps of Wood on that side of the Tide came furiously in, without doubt the water would have swept them away."

Appendix
Mughal Painting

Patrons: the Mughal Emperors

Babur	932-37/1526-30
Humayun	937-47/1530-40; 962-63/1555-56
Akbar	963-1014/1556-1605
Jahangir	1014-37/1605-27
Shah Jahan	1037-68/1628-57
Aurangzeb	1068-1118/1658-1707
	[Witnessed the decline of Mughal School]

The Mughal School of painting, considered to be a creation of Akbar, developed during 16th and 17th centuries under the patronage of the Mughal emperors, princes and nobles. It has won the recognition of the art-historians and connoisseurs for the art of book-illustration and portraiture. Mughal artists' contribution is highly commended for their pictures containing evidence on day to day activities and wildlife. The genre pictures from this school are equally important since these are invaluable records of cultural history. In fact, the Mughal painting moves around the historical subjects of painting and actual portraits of human-beings, birds, animals and flowers, etc. Depiction of these subjects with scientific precision is the basic concept of reality portrayed by the Mughal artists. In this regard, no other school, either Persian or pre-Muhammadan Indian painting excel Mughal painters' work. The most significant aspect of the Mughal school is the historical nature of the abundant dated material available from this centre in a consequent manner. Further, it shows a continuity of the various traits of art, viz., Ajanta art, Buddhist or Eastern India school and Jain or Western India school besides the impact of Persian and Renaissance Art. Lastly, the development of various branches of art, i.e., historical portraits, self-portraiture, zoological pictures and margin-painting which reached to its zenith at the Mughal atelier, while opened new chapters in Indian art history, also provided new areas of painting for future generation. Need not say manuscript painting, portraiture and illumination work attained great perfection and became livelier and active than the past.

The Mughal school is not essentially the heritage of the past, and its rise with the innovations and novelties is distinct in the history of world art. Large impact of the Mughal school is well-evidenced on the eighteenth-nineteenth centuries Indian schools such as those flourished at Oudh (Lucknow and Faizabad), Lahore, Delhi and Patna. It also influenced the Rajasthani and Hill centres of painting, Sikh painting and the schools of South India. It further influenced allied forms of decorative arts.

Babur (1526-1530), the first ruler of the Mughal dynasty, was a naturalist and had a vision of an art critic. He says of the famous Persian master painter Bihzad that "His work was very dainty but he did not draw beardless faces well, he used greatly to lengthen the double chin (*ghab ghab*), bearded faces he drew admirably".[1] Of another famous Persian painter, Shah Muzaffar, he writes that 'he painted dainty portraits, representing the hair very daintly'.[2]

Humayun, while fugitive, came into direct contact of the Persian painters active at Shah Tahmasp court in 1544. Humayun utilized his forced sojourn at the Safavid court to gather notable Iranian painters around him. A recent finding of a manuscript of the *Khamsa* of Nizami, datable 1550-54, and preserved in Bibliotheque nationale de France, Paris (Smith-Lesouef 216) further enriches the wealth of painting known to have been executed under Humayun at Kabul.[3] Its illustrations, bereft of Indian elements, exhibit an amalgam of Tabrizi and Bukharan elements. In order of chronology, the illustrations of another copy of *Khamsa* of Nizami, now in Kasturbhai and Lalbhai Collection, Ahmedabad were executed in India during 1556.[4] In all it contains 34 miniatures of which 17 are distinctly Persian (11 in Bukharan style; 6 are affiliated with the Safavid style of Tabriz), and the remaining betray a mixture of Indian and Persian styles. Of course, these illustrations have no uniformity of style, and in them varying trends influencing the early Mughal painters' work can be seen. The Fitzwilliam Album—a scrapbook of painting and calligraphies—also belongs to Humayun's court.[5] The paintings of Humayun's period are dominated by the traditions of Persian art. The Persian master painters: Maulana Dost Masauwir, Maulana Darvish Muhammad, Maulana Yusuf, Mir Musauwir (or Mir Mansur), Mir Sayyid Ali and Khwaja Abdu-s Samad introduced trends and techniques of Persian painting at Humayun's atelier and they synthesized the traditions of Turkoman Tabriz and Timurid Herat. These painters greatly contributed to the evolution of the Persianized school of Indian art, which matured as the Mughal school.

One of the earliest and most remarkable artistic projects at Akbar's atelier was the *Hamzanama* (*ca.* 1562-80). Mulla Alauddaula Qazwini tells us in his *Nafais-al Maasir* (1573) that fifty painters worked on this project under the surpervision of Mir Sayyid Ali who left for the pilgrimage to Mecca by the time its first four illustrated volumes were completed. The remaining part of this voluminous work was put under the supervision of Khwaja Abdu-s Samad.[6] This project took 15 years to complete.[7] Abu'l Fazl has noted that it comprised 12 volumes and illustrated no less than one thousand and four hundred passages of the exploits of Amir Hamza, an uncle of Prophet Muhammad.[8] Akbar listened its passages describing unreal episodes for delight and pleasure, recited by his reader Mulla Inayat 'Durbar Khan'.[9]

The *Hamzanama* illustrations most likely belonged to the tradition of tent hangings, or temple hangings called *pichhais*. These are executed on cloth on an unprecedented scale exceeding in size to any other known Indian book-painting.[10] It is thus described by Arif Qandahari:

> One of the curious events is that His Majesty ordered the story of Amir Hamza, consisting of 360 tales, should be illustrated, inclusive of the "assemblies" (*majalis*) so that a hundred unique painters, gilders, decorators and binders work in the making of that book. The size of that book is one and a half *gaz-i shari*, the paper is coloured and the margin gold-sprinkled [?] (*jalkari*), and between every two sheets of paper, muslin (*chautar*) cloth is inserted for better strength. All the pages contain pictures and gilding. It was ordered that writers of excellent style should read the tales and put them in suitable and proper prose, which then should be transcribed by skilled scribes. Despite this

[effort], a volume takes one year to prepare, and on each volume about two lakh copper *tankas* are spent.[11]

Though none of the *Hamza* illustrations bear the artist's name, these have been attributed variously to Mir Sayyid Ali, Khwaja Abdu-s Samad, Basawan and Daswant.

The style of the *Hamza* illustrations is far more innovative and bear evidence of definite links between the Persian and Indian schools. In them the flat depiction of architectural columns comprising profuse embellishment in jewel-like manner, intricate geometric patterns, use of limited palette of bright pigments, and composition in symmetrical order show affinity with the Safavid school. In *Hamza* illustrations, the function of colour is purely decorative. However, the forms depicted in illustrations are not bereft of naturalism and rhythmic movement, which pronounce Indian trends of art. Here, the typical treatment of the picture space with an arrangement of plane behind plane, i.e., subsidiary scenes set in the background, is fundamentally Indian. Further, in the numerous illustrations, the treatment of trees is typically Indian where foliage is painted with dark background. Moreover, the luxuriant depiction of foliage with brilliant blossoms is derived from the Deccan painting of India. It is notable that an extraordinary vigour of action and violent movement seen in several illustrations of the *Hamza* is altogether absent in pre-Mughal art book in India and in the art of Persia as well. It was something new, which bore the signs of the Mughal painter's originality, and also marked the appearance of a new style, i.e., Mughal. It is important that Persian trends (Safavid and Timurid) did not make progress in their purest form; and these did not remain uninfluenced by the Indian traditions, particularly the vigorous realism of the Rajasthani school. The glimpses of purely Indian inspiration in *Hamza* illustrations, e.g., "women at the well" is a straight-forward derivation of an early Rajasthani painting (Pl. 27).[12]

The impact of the Renaissance art, too, begins to be seen in Mughal art by the 1570s. In *Hamza* illustrations, the technique of shading employed to create a three-dimensional effect with physical form and substance, not known in the Persian and Indian miniatures of the time, is an adaptation of European methods of painting. These show a rudimentary knowledge of humanistic painting revealing the technique of shading to represent mass and volume. There is also seen an advance towards appreciation of perspective where the human figures and the distant buildings in the background appear comparatively diminutive in size as compared to those in the foreground to emphasize depth in painting.

Mir Sayyid Ali (Safavid school) and Khwaja Abdu-s Samad (Shiraz school), who surpervised the earliest project—illustration of the *Hamzanama*, left their impress on the early Mughal school, and to a great extent formulated the narrative modes of the art of book-illustration in Mughal style. Besides, painters from Bukhara, Herat and Kabul were active at the imperial Mughal atelier: the most distinguished amongst them are Farrukh Beg, Aqa Riza and Farrukh Qalmaq (of Mongol origin). Their style and technique not only shaped the Mughal style, but also inspired the artistic expression in general for at least two centuries. Persian elements became an integral part of the Mughal painting: and no Mughal painting can be explained without a knowledge of the Persian schools of art. Even so, the Mughal school should not be considered a mere offshoot of the traditions of Persian painting; in fact it is always possible to distinguish a Mughal from a Persian painting.

The development of the Mughal painting is credited to Akbar's characteristic enthusiasm and love for the art of painting right from his childhood. Abu'l Fazl writes:

> His Majesty, from his earliest youth, has shown a great predilection for this art, and gives it every encouragement, as he looks upon it as a means, both of study and amusement. Hence the art flourishes, and many painters have obtained great reputation.[13]

A record of each painter's work was kept at the atelier to check his progress:

> The work of all painters are weekly laid before His Majesty by the *Daroghas* and the clerks; he then confers rewards according to excellence of workmanship, or increase the monthly salaries.[14]

For the first time, a conscious effort was made under Akbar to rescue painting from religious connotations. He marshalled a subtle philosophical argument against the Islamic theological disapproval of painting:

> Bigoted followers of the letter of the law are hostile to the art of painting; but their eyes now see the truth. One day at a private party of friends, His Majesty, who had conferred on several the pleasure of drawing near him, remarked: "There are many that hate painting; but such men I dislike. It appears to me as if a painter had quite peculiar means of recognizing God; for a painter in sketching anything that has life, and in devising its limbs, one after the other, must come to feel that he cannot bestow individuality upon his work, and is thus forced to think of God, the giver of life, and will thus increase in knowledge.[15]

Akbar's dominant interest in painting was related to its thematic aspects rather than its ideological or spiritual dimensions. At Akbar's atelier there was no attempt to ascribe divine attributes to any individual through pictorial symbolism. It was only during the seventeenth century that the portraits of the Mughal emperors were given haloes, cherubs, angels, etc. to signify their proximity to divinity. These figurative motifs, directly adopted from the Renaissance art of Europe, were utilized by the painters of Jahangir and Shah Jahan for apotheosis portraits of their royal patrons. Akbar preferred the historical portraits imbibing innate characters of the subjects. So great was Akbar's anxiety to have his authentic portraits made that he especially sat for the painter, who drew his likeness; and ordered for an album of portraits of his grandees to be prepared.[16] For Akbar, the painter's work explored both external and internal qualities of an object. This is highlighted by Abu'l Fazl's remark regarding Khwaja Abdu-s Samad:

> Though he was skilled in art of painting before joining Mughal service, by the Emperor's insight he achieved a high station, and from bringing out mere forms he came to bring out the inner meaning.[17]

In India, the patrons generally looked for the subjects of painting of a kind, overwhelmingly religious texts. New themes of painting other than the religious emerged first in the fifteenth century Malwa painting (Mandu school), and the illustrations of the MSS *Ni'matnama* (Cookery Book) and *Miftah-ul Fuzala* (a Persian Lexicon) opened the way to a fresh conceptual and stylistic expression in art (Pls. 25, 29, 34, 37-38 & 70-72). Akbar as a patron, discovered new themes for painting which encompassed Islamic, Indian and European themes and accommodated religious, historical and non-historical subjects. The choice of themes for paintings at Akbar's atelier was also influenced by his liberal and tolerant attitude towards the religions other than Islam, i.e., Hinduism and Christianity. A good number of Hindu epics, e.g., *Harivamsha, Mahabharata, Panchatantra, Ramayana*, etc. were translated into Persian and these translations were often illustrated with pictures. Asaf Khan Jafar Beg writes in the introduction of *Tarikh-i Alfi*:

> His heart is inclined to justice, desiring that the followers of different faith, each having become acquainted with the truth and reality of others' religion, should act with restraint and abandon bigotry. He has accordingly ordered that the rational contents of different religions and faiths should be translated in the language of each, and that the rose garden of the traditional aspects of each religion should as far as possible, be cleared of the thorns of bigotry.[18]

There appeared an attempt at making courtiers conversant with Indian cultural values. Akbar is reported to have asked his nobles to acquire the copies of the *Razmnama* (Persian translation of the *Mahabharata*), decorated with pictures. Similarly, the *Dastan-i Masih* ('Life of Christ'), a Persian translation of a work in Portuguese, based on the Gospels was repeatedly illustrated at Akbar's atelier, in addition to the preparation of numerous copies of European pictures and engravings on Biblical themes, most notably by the artist Kesavdas.

The role of patron always proved vital in the formation of the Mughal school. Jahangir's unending passion for historical portraits, nature and wildlife promoted portraiture and pictures on nature and history; and Shah Jahan's innate love for surface brilliance and ornate objects drew the artist's work very close to that of a skilled draftsman. Subsequently, in the latter's reign, the most luxurious phase of Mughal painting began as judged from the richness of ornamentation and technical perfection.

Similarly, Mughal patrons' interest in European pictures immediately influenced the work of Mughal artists. The impact was so great that the seventeenth century Mughal painting cannot be studied without a knowledge of Renaissance art. Direct imitation of European pictures, adaptation and incorporation of their technical features and symbolism became a constant feature of the Mughal school, where the painters, viz., Basawan, La'l, Kesavdas, Miskin, Abu'l Hasan, Bichitr, Govardhan, Manohar and Payag, who attained great fame and are reckoned as great masters, largely fulfilled the demand of their patrons. The linear art of Persia alone did not fascinate the Mughal connoisseurs and painters. The Mughal artists, under the influence of the Renaissance humanist movement in art, added a new chapter in Indian art which is neither a direct continuation of the pre-Islamic Indian traditions and nor explicitly Persian. The Mughal painting, eclectic in character, evolved with the interaction of various traditions predominantly Indian, Persian and European. The context of naturalism, scientific perspective and *chiaroscuro*—contrasts in light and shade in Mughal painting—is the gift of humanism as practised by the European artists of Renaissance.

The Mughal school is thus fundamentally different from its precursors in that here an artist's goal appears to be the portrayal of the objective reality and the presentation of nature with an almost photographic fidelity—the very tenets of Renaissance art. An artist was now expected to work from memory by looking at the subject and not from imagination. Thus, the portrait, bird and animal pictures, flower painting and naturalistic drawings of the plants with blossom in margin-decoration produced at the Mughal atelier differed from the archetypes of the past. The portraits of ordinary people, in general, are spontaneous pictures, altogether different from the stately ones of the royalty or nobles, which often appear mannered and idealized. The formalized expression, however, does not effect the sensitive rendering of characteristic features of the subject. Undoubtedly, Mughal artists achieved great success in executing truly life-like images of their subjects by absorbing elements of Renaissance humanism in their art; and indeed a few Mughal masters, viz., Basawan, Bichitr, Daulat, Govardhan, Mirar and Payag could even reach the acumen of great Renaissance artists.

In this context, the striking portraits of Shah Jahan ascribed respectively to Bichitr and Payag from the Chester Beatty Library deserve a mention. Bichitr's portrait of Shah Jahan (*ca.* 1635) excels both in its idealization and in the use of symbols.[19] In it, the figure of Shah Jahan is prominently depicted with a large radiating halo, standing on a terrestrial globe with the conventional symbol of 'lion and sheep' and the two angels descending amidst billowing clouds and holding the royal insignia (a European crown). In addition, on either side of the subject there are two groups of holy men emerging from the clouds with their hands lifted in prayer, diminutive with details deliberately blurred. Here while most symbolism comes right out of the conventions of European painting practically unaltered, the introduction of the holy men in groups—the Muslim theologians, amidst clouds—is an innovation of Bichitr. It certainly enriches the visual vocabulary of symbols in Mughal iconography. Lastly, the representation of a noble, shown perceptibly small in size, with a sword hung around his neck—a symbolic representation of an individual's surrender in the east—at the bottom towards the right corner again testifies to Bichitr's ingenuity in the application of symbols. In another portrait (*ca.* 1635-7), also at the Chester Beatty Library, ascribed to Payag, the emperor is shown standing on a terrestrial globe holding a matchlock.[20] The background comprises horsemen storming a fort and a group of men presenting themselves before the Emperor, all depicted on a drastically reduced scale and blurred in effect. The artist's understanding of the aerial perspective is here in full accordance of Renaissance art. By now, the mode of drawing the main character much larger than the other objects seems to have become the mainstay of the Mughal artists in the presentation of royal or aristocratic portraits.

One must here realise that the adoption of Renaissance humanism in Mughal art was not the result of an intellectual or scientific movement; and this certainly handicapped it in appreciating the full force of Europe's achievement in art. Mughal painters could not, after all, liberate themselves from the canons of the conventional art of Persia and India, though their conscious effort to switch over to the methods and techniques of Renaissance art showed both skill and ingenuity.

Mughal patrons' special emphasis on the delineation of the characteristic details served as an essential basis of the development of portraiture, which embraced historical and psychological elements of art. Jahangir, like his father, had portraits made of his nobles, which he gathered together in albums. This emerges from an anecdote narrated in the *Zakhiratu'l Khawanin*.[21] While looking at the portraits of the nobles, Jahangir passed some remarks on 'Abdulla Khan, Safi Khan and Rana Ramdas who had not served well in the Deccan. As against these nobles, 'Ali Mardan Khan had performed commendable; so the Emperor ordered his portrait to be included in the *Jahangirnama*.

Jahangir had portraits made not only of the nobles of his court but of Safavid and Uzbek rulers and nobles as well. He writes:

> At the time [1613] when I sent Khan 'Alam to Persia, I had sent with him a painter of the name Bishandas, who was unequalled in his age for taking likeness, to take the portraits of the Shah and the chiefmen of his State, and bring them. He had drawn the likeness of most of them and especially had taken that of my brother the Shah exceedingly well, so that, when I showed it to any of his servants, they said it was exceedingly well drawn (account of the year 1618).[22]

Jahangir took care to check the authenticity of the portraits with those who had seen the person portrayed. A Central Asian scholar Mutribi, who visited his court in 1626, informs how Jahangir strove to secure accuracy in the portraits he was collecting:

> Today the Emperor showed me the pictures of Uzbek Khans. I recognized 'Abul Be there.[23]
>
> ...
>
> I presented myself before the Emperor. His Majesty was holding a paper bearing a picture in his hand and was looking at the picture. Favouring me with his attention, he called me near him and said, 'See these pictures. Do you know whose portraits (*surat*) they are'? When I looked at them, I found that one was the portrait of 'Abdulla Khan Uzbek and the other of 'Abdul Momin Khan. His Majesty said, 'Are they really their likenesses (*shabih*) or do you have some comment to make? If you have some comment do speak out'. I said, 'The portrait of 'Abdulla Khan shows him as plump and his beard has been shown as straight. He was not like this. He had little flesh on his body and his beard tended to incline to one side'. His Majesty asked, 'Was the inclination of the beard to the right or to the left'? I said, 'To the left'. His Majesty summoned the painter (*musauwir*) and whatever I had

> said he repeated that to him. Thereafter he said, 'Have you got anything to say on the likeness of 'Abdul Momin Khan'? I said, 'The artist has shown 'Abdul Momin Khan as of dark complexion. But he was not like this. His dark complexion was inclined towards fairness and he tied his turban's sash (*ilaqa'*) in front, two fists in length. It looked very well'. His Majesty said, 'Take off your turban and show us how his turban's sash looked'. I took off my turban and showed how it was made. His Majesty told the artist, 'Make your picture this way'. The next day the artist brought his pictures drawn in the way that I had indicated. This won His Majesty's approval. 'Abul Be Uzbek, known as Bahadur Khan being present, said, 'When I was a servant of 'Abdul Momin Khan, he did not wear the turban's sash (like this)'. The Emperor said, 'The *akhund* (present author) is referring to the time when he ('Abdul Momin Khan) was a prince, i.e., 15 years of age.[24]

The Mughal Emperors, princes and nobles further showed interest in holy men, whether Muslim or Hindu. It so appears from the genre pictures depicting emperors, princes and others visiting ascetics. The miniature "Jahangir visiting the ascetic Gosai Jadrup" (*ca.* 1616-20)[25] corroborates the emperor's account in his *Memoirs* (Pl. 8):

> I had frequently heard that an austere Sannyasi of the name of Jadrup many years ago retired from the city of Ujjain to a corner of the desert and employed himself in the worship of the true God. I had a great desire for his acquaintance, ... When I arrived in the neighbourhood of the city I alighted from the boat and went ½ kos on foot to see him. The place he had chosen to live in was a hole on the side of a hill which had been dug out and a door made. At the entrance there is an opening in the shape of a *mihrab*, which is in length (?height) 1 gaz and in breadth 10 *gira* (knots, each 1/12 of a gaz), and the distance from this door to a hole which is his real abode is in length 5 knots in length and in breadth 11½ knots. The height from the ground to the roof is 1 gaz and 3 knots. ... It has no mat and no straw. In this narrow and dark hole he passes his time in solitude. In the cold days of winter, though he is quite naked, with the exception of a piece of rag that he has in front and behind, he never lights a fire.[26]

In another instance, several miniatures show Dara Shikoh visiting ascetics. It is notable that in a Mughal picture, besides the detail of the painting, the significance of its subject, too, is relevant. It lends the Mughal painting a quality of biographical record.

The images in these miniatures are fully authentic and with no sign of an idealized or flattering image. This realistic approach to the subject can be seen in a series of pictures of the ordinary men and ascetics, etc. Need not say the 'realism' evinced in the Mughal painters' work determine the golden age of the Mughal painting. Jahangiri painters successfully explored the individuality of the figures revealing their personalities. Beach has to say that "Jahangiri paintings intend a straightforward naturalism, a belief that is the character of the subject, ... Painting was a way of exploring the external world of reality which was momentarily unquestioned."[27]

The Mughal portraits, in general, reveal some insight into character. The images are painted with wealth of emotion and are the masterpieces of creative art, never surpassed in medieval India. Here a caveat to the historicity of the Mughal portraiture may be entered in relation to the portraits of royal harem ladies that all their representations are ideal types, and that they were not drawn from life.

Jahangir, too, personally examined the work of his painters; and by looking at the miniatures executed by them had acquired the knowledge of their style, and could recognize their work without the artist's name being told to him.

> As regards myself, my liking for painting and my practice in judging it have arrived at such a point that when any work is brought before me, either of deceased artists or those of the present day, without the names being told me, I say on the spur of moment that it is the work of such and such a man. And if there be a picture containing many portraits, and each face be the work of a different

> master, I can discover which face is the work of each of them. If any other person has put in the eye and eyebrow of a face, I can perceive whose work the original face is, and who has painted the eye and eyebrows.[28]

Jahangir considered the painting as a source of historical documentation of the rarities of nature, and peculiar and strange events from day to day life. This basic approach to the subject of painting was to generate the feel of the past and present. Let us hear Jahangir:

> As these animals appeared to me to be very strange. I both described them and ordered the painters should draw them in the *Jahangirnama* so that the amazement that arose from hearing of them might be increased.[29]

In another instance he writes:

> At this time the king of Persia had sent with Pari Beg Mir Shikar (chief huntsman) one falcon (shunqar) of good colour. ...Though it was brought to court, it did not live more than a week.... As it was something out of common, I ordered Ustad Mansur, who has the title of *Nadiru-l 'Asr* (Wonder of the Age) to paint and preserve its likeness.[30]

In the Mughal school, next to human portraiture, the important subject of painting is the study of birds, animals and flowers. Jahangir's curiosity in natural history was rather intense, and he wanted to see greater likeness in the representation of wild life. His enthusiasm for knowledge of natural history was further sharpened by his almost scientific curiosity, which was enough reason for his foremost preference for specialization in art, and then, precision in recapturing the exact likeness of the living objects of nature. Most exclusive pictures of wild life executed under his patronage clearly show that the Mughal school owes its highest achievement to this aesthete Emperor.

Under Shah Jahan (1628-1658), in general, the portraiture still held a prominent place. An apotheosis portrait of the emperor and the equestrian portraits received attention of the artists. Besides, the assumed picture of Akbar, Jahangir and Shah Jahan in a group emerged as a typified composition. The portrayal of ascetics and saints further won painters' sympathy. Shah Jahan's attitude towards painting, though accommodated earlier Mughal trends of aesthetics, showed an explicit emphasis on the perfect idealization imbued with striking ornamentation, brilliant colour effect and plentiful details. As a result of it, the humanistic elements, viz., naturalism and psychological insight evidenced in Jahangiri paintings became inconspicuous. This departure in Mughal style from naturalism to an idealized reality rather encouraged a forged representation in art. Thus, Shah Jahan's viewpoint endorsed a dissimilar aesthetic in Mughal painting, which proved a halting point and the style became static and represented its proper culmination. Beach finds a retreat from Jahangiri naturalism in various Shah Jahan period works. According to him, they really represent the proper culmination of the Mughal style, for which the achievements of painting under Jahangir were indispensable.[31] Pratapaditya Pal sums up Shah Jahan's phase of painting thus: "Style rather than substance, outward appearance rather than inner character, decorative exuberance rather than restraint, technical virtuosity rather than spontaneous expressiveness are some of the salient features of Shah Jahani painting."[32]

The margin-painting, developed at the Mughal school as an integral part of the art of the book and album pictures basically inspired by the Persian art (especially Safavid and Timurid schools), reached its zenith at Jahangir's studio with the introduction of wide margins accommodating cartouches and medallions; these were featured amid foliage with birds and animals, genre scenes and naturalistic flower-plants with blossom executed on the untouched background, i.e., buff-shade of the paper, in light gouache and in gold of different shades to suggest modelling and shading. Notably, the margins comprising careful drawings of flower plants with botanical details, images of nobles, artisans and professionals, artists and others rendered in colour or tints have no parallel in the art of Safavid Iran and pre-Mughal art of India.

It is notable that in Indian art, signed and ascribed miniatures are known first from Akbar's atelier. This practice of artist's name being given on his works made it possible to recognize an artist as an individual and assess his achievement. That being so, each artist had an opportunity to bring out his characteristic originality making him conscious of his individuality. Thus, possibly the ground was prepared for ushering individualism in his art.

Furthermore, the significant development of self-portrait painting at the Mughal school has its continuity in the mid-eighteenth century Rajasthani and Hill schools of painting.[33]

Aurangzeb's (1658-1707) reign is not known for encouragement to painting; and the glorious chapter of the Mughal artists' achievements was abruptly and unexpectedly cut short due to his indifference to the art of painting. The great period of patronage and achievement in Mughal painting was over. However, at least during the early years of his reign, royal atelier was in function. Bernier (1656-1658) describes the atelier as a part of the Imperial workshops:

> Large halls are seen in many places, called *Karkanays* or workshops for the artisans. In one hall embroiderers are busily employed, superintended by a master. In another you see the goldsmiths; in a third, painters; in a fourth varnishers in lacquer—work, in a fifth, joiners, turners, tailors, and shoe-makers; in a sixth, manufacturers of silk, brocades, and those fine muslins of which are made turbans, girdles with golden flowers, and drawers worn by females, so delicately fine as frequently to wear out in one night.[34]

With the decline of Imperial and aristocratic patronage, there is witnessed a decay of the art. This at least seems to have been the view of two contemporary European travellers. Bernier writes:

> I have often admired the beauty, softness, and delicacy of their paintings and miniatures, and was particularly struck with the exploits of *Ekbar*, painted on a shield by a celebrated artist, who is said to have been seven years in completing the picture. I thought it a wonderful performance. The *Indian* painters are chiefly deficient in just proportions, and in the expression of the face; but these defects would soon be corrected if they possessed good masters, and were instructed in the rules of art.
>
> Want of genius, therefore is not the reason why works of superior art are not exhibited in the capital. If the artists and manufacturers were encouraged, the useful and fine arts would flourish; but these unhappy men are condemned, with harshness, and inadequately remunerated for their labour.[35]

Thevenot (1666-67) makes a similar observation:

> Order is observed in them, the Personages have the suitableness that is necessary in them, and the colours are very lovely, but they make Faces ill. They do thing in miniature pretty well, and there are some at *Dehly* who Engrave indifferently well also; but seeing they are not much encouraged, they do not apply themselves to their work, with all the exactness they might, and all their craft is to do as much work as they can, for present Money to subsist on.[36]

Thevenot also refers to the sale of paintings in the bazaars of Agra and Delhi:

> One may see a great many pictures in the Indies upon Paper and Paste-Board, but generally they are dull pieces, and none are esteemed but those of *Agra* and *Dehly*. However, since those of *Agra* are for the most part, indecent, and represent Lacivious Postures, worse than those of Aretin, there are but few civil Europeans that will by them.[37]

A note on an eclectic character of the Mughal painting is relevant since eclecticism has been looked upon as a sign of decadence. It betrays a cultural poverty, whether of craftsmanship or originality. Havell observes that "an endeavour to assimilate European ideas is nearly always disastrous to the oriental artist, on account of the opposition between his views of life and of Nature and those which govern Western art".[38] He further writes:

> A curious instance of this is to be found in the work of a Persian artist of the early seventeenth century, who was sent to Europe by Shah Abbas to study painting in Rome. His pictures, some of which are now preserved in the British Museum, reveal a hopeless conflict between his subconscious views of art and his painful effort to show things as he was wanted to show them; the result being, on the one hand, the total loss of what was valuable in his own art, and, on the other, a complete failure to reproduce anything of artistic value in his translation of European art. However, Havell notices an introduction of landscape backgrounds to figure-subjects with effects of chiaroscuro seen in Mughal painting reveal a complete understanding of the true function of the fine art.[39] Rogers, too, observes that the Mughal painters' recourse of modelling, stereoscopic perspective and the use of *sfumato* and other European techniques to convey distance by colour gradations is, however, even more marked in the treatment of themes of non-European origin, including natural history of painting for Jahangir; ...There is, therefore, little evidence for the conclusion that eclecticism in Mughal art—whether of style or source material, either because the painters had no option but to take second-rate models which happened to come their way or because they were unable to combine incompatible elements into an artistically productive style—brought a decline in quality. On the contrary it was precisely the fusion of styles—Indian, Persian and European—which gave Mughal painting its individuality and force'.[40]

In this connection, an outstanding talent amongst the individuals, Abu'l Hasan, Balchand Basawan, Daulat, Bichitr, Govardhan, Manohar, Payag, etc. is discovered. Their eclectic art represented the painting which was not experienced before in India or Iran. Okada observes that Abu'l Hasan acquired a taste for naturalism and a sense of volume and perspective from the study of European engravings, which led him eventually to break with Safavid school.[41] She further writes that Payag's chiaroscuro effects were totally alien to Indo-Persian pictorial tradition, and were apparently inspired by European models.[42] The techniques of light and shadow, realistic setting and scientific perspective were wholly alien from the Indian and Persian conventions. The reverence for the physical reality observed in the European art had no place in classical art of India and Persia. The spirit of romance pervading the Persian painting, and the overwhelmingly idealized art of India is just opposite to the fundamentals of reality of 15th, 16th and 17th centuries art of Europe.

The tenets of High Mughal style (first quarter of 17th century) heavily burdened with the concept of 'physical reality' are not in harmony with the trends of Indian art; or say, are alien. Havell has rightly remarked:

> The academic tradition of Hindu and Buddhist sculpture and painting was, and is still, entirely based on symbolism, and without the knowledge of interpreting it no one can enter deeply into the study of any branch of Indian art.... The gulf which divides East and West is that which separates realism from idealism.... India insists that what we call reality is deceptive and untruthful, and strives to express it through the ideal.[43]

Beach observes: "... for the Hindu ideal was to find what was universal, rather than particular, in a world of impermanence and illusion. The Mughal concern for objective distinctness and human individuality was therefore a radical shift from within both Islamic and Indian traditions."[44]

Consequently, Beach has to say that though thematic trends and techniques of European art incorporated in Mughal paintings made it popular and comprehensible as well in Europe (The sensitive naturalism in Mughal painting suited much to the taste of European), these must have remained foreign exoticisms to viewers in India at the time.[45]

One finds Mughal painting heavily indebted to European art during the course of its development and maturity. This impact was so great that Mughal painting has been looked upon as a 'hybrid blend' of East and West. In the Mughal style, it is seen that with the gradual rise of impact of Renaissance art, there was a shrinkage in the development of both Indian and Persian themes and techniques. In a way Mughal painting, harnessed with the tenets of Renaissance art, discredited oriental Persian and Indian art. Hodgson finds that Akbar's interest in European works went far beyond the production of exact copies. Instead, foreign techniques were made subservient to the Mughal ideals being expressed and explored.[46] Akbar's concept of painting promoted realism and brushed aside the basics of Safavid and Timurid paintings.[47] His great success in this direction is claimed by Abu'l Fazl who writes: "[Mughal masterpieces] may be placed at the side of the wonderful works of the European painters who have attained world-wide fame;"[48] "even inanimate objects look as if they had life."[49] Pratapaditya Pal infers that this statement of Abu'l Fazl clearly demonstrates how European painting had replaced Persian painting as a measure of excellence.[50] Obviously, the tenets of Indian and Persian painting became weak and a new eclectic art generated. An emphasis on the 'realism' was so great that sometimes Mughal masters retouched and overpainted stereotyped and inexpressive faces shown in the Persian miniatures. Bishandas retouched the human faces in the work of Persian master's work, probably by Aqa Mirak of Isfahan—a painter of Shah Tahmasp's court (1514-1576), and a pupil of Bihzad (active about 1480-1535 or 1536). Okada writes that the new faces that sprang from the brush of the Mughal painters were markedly more realistic.[51] It is also true in case of the figures overpainted in the famous Mughal picture 'The House of Timur' (*ca.*1552-54) during Jahangir's time.[52]

NOTES

1. *Baburnama* (Turki text: 1530), tr. A.S. Beveridge, New Delhi, Reprint, 1979, p. 291.
2. Ibid.
3. C. Adle, "New Data on the Dawn of Mughal Painting and Calligraphy" in Muzaffar Alam, Francoise 'Nalini' Delvoye and Marc Gaborieau, eds. *The Making of Indo-Persian Culture, Indian and French Studies*, New Delhi, 2000, pp. 208-09, pls. 11-3.
4. Ibid., pp. 209-10.
5. M.C. Beach, *Early Mughal Painting*, New York, 1987, fig. 33; also in his *The New Cambridge History of India: Mughal and Rajput Painting*, Cambridge, 1992, pp. 19, 21-2, figs. 9-10 and 12.
6. Mulla Alaud-Daula Qazwini, *Nafais-al Maasir* (1573), text, f.52a.
7. Abdul Qadir Badaoni, *Muntakhabu-t Tawarikh* (1595), tr. II, p. 292.
8. *A'in-i Akbari* (1595), tr. I, p. 115; Badaoni, op. cit., writes that the illustrated *Hamzanama* was completed in 16 volumes.
9. Abu'l Fazl, *Akbarnama* (1601), tr. II, pp. 434-4.
10. Badaoni (op. cit.) records that each page of it measures a yard wide and a yard long, and on each page is a picture. Also see Shah Nawaz Khan, *Maasir-ul Umara (1742-80)*, tr. I, p. 454 where he writes that Akbar was very fond of the story of Amir Hamza which contained 360 tales. So much so that he in the female apartments used to recite them like a storyteller. He had the wonderful incidents of that story illustrated from beginning to end of the book and set up in twelve volumes.
11. Haji Muhammad 'Arif Qandhari, *Tarikh-i Akbari* (1580), ed. text, p. 45.
12. Basil Gray, *Rajput Painting*, London, no date, pl. 2 (Rajasthani detail from an illustration to the *Hamzanama*).

13. Abu'l Fazl, *Ain-i Akbari*, ed. text, p. 116, tr. Vol. I, p. 113.
14. Ibid.
15. Ibid., ed. text, p. 118, tr. Vol. I, pp. 114-5.
16. Ibid.
17. Ibid.
18. See Sayyid Athar Abbas Rizvi, *Religious and Intellectual History of the Muslims in Akbar's Reign (1556-1605)*, New Delhi, 1975, p. 254.
19. S.P. Verma, *Mughal Painters and Their Work: A Biographical Survey and Comprehensive Catalogue*, New Delhi, 1994, pl. XXI. pp. 106-07.
20. Amina Okada, *Imperial Mughal Painters, Indian Miniatures from the Sixteenth and Seventeenth Centuries*, tr. Deke Dusinberre, Flammarion, no date, p. 208, fig. 247.
21. *Zakhiratu'l Khawanin* of Shah Farid Bhakkari, ed. Sayed Moinul Haq, Karachi, 1961, pp. 47-8.
22. *Tuzuk-i Jahangiri*, ed. text, p. 275, tr. II, pp. 116-7.
23. Mutribi, *Khatirat-i Mutribi Samarqandi*, ed. Abdul Ghani Mirzoyef, Karachi, 1977, p. 61.
24. Ibid., pp. 61-2.
25. Okada, op. cit., fig. 40.
26. *Tuzuk-i Jahangiri*, tr. I, pp. 355-56.
27. M.C. Beach, *The Grand Mogul: Imperial Painting in India (1600-1660)*, Williamstown, Mass, 1978, p. 27.
28. *Tuzuk-i Jahangiri*, ed. text, p. 235, tr. II, pp. 20-1.
29. Ibid., ed. text, p. 105, tr. I, p. 215.
30. Ibid., ed. text, pp. 280-1, tr. II, pp. 107-8.
31. Beach, *The Grand Mogul*, & C., op. cit., p. 29.
32. Pratapaditya Pal, *Indian Painting: A Catalogue of the Los Angeles County Museum of Art Collection*, California, 1993, p. 185.
33. S.P. Verma, *Painting the Mughal Experience*, New Delhi, 2005, pp. 77-80, fig. 11.
34. Francois Bernier, *Travels in the Mughal Empire, 1656-58*, tr. A. Constable, revised by V.A. Smith, London, 1916, pp. 258-59.
35. Ibid., pp. 254-55.
36. M. de Thevenot, *Indian Travels of Thevenot and Careri*, ed. S. Sen, New Delhi, 1949, p. 65.
37. Ibid., p. 55.
38. E.B. Havell, *Indian Sculpture and Painting*, London, 1908, p. 219.
39. Ibid., pp. 219-20.
40. J.M. Rogers, *Mughal Miniatures*, London, 1993, p. 106.
41. Okada, op. cit., pp. 171-72.
42. Ibid., p. 211.
43. E.B. Havell, "The Symbolism in Indian Sculpture and Painting", *The Burlington Magazine*, Vol. XV, No. LXXVIII, London, 1909, p. 345.
44. Beach, *Mughal and Rajput Painting*, op. cit., p. 136.
45. Ibid., p. 105.
46. Hodgson Marshall, *The Ventures of Islam*, Vol. III, Chicago, 1974, p. 76.
47. M. Brand and G.D. Lowry, *Akbar's India: Art from the Mughal City of Victory*, New York, 1985, p. 127.
48. *Ain-i Akbari*, op. cit., p. 113.
49. Ibid., pp. 113-14.
50. Pal, op. cit., p. 180.
51. Okada, op. cit., p. 174.
52. John Seyller, "Recycled Images: Overpainting in Early Mughal Art" in S.C. Canby, ed. *Humayun's Garden Party, Princes of the House of Timur and Early Mughal Painting*, Mumbai, 1994, figs. 6, 8-9.

Bibliography

The Bibliography is divided into two parts. Part I lists the illustrated MSS and albums of Mughal miniatures with particulars of the collections to which they belong, and the number of miniatures contained in each. Stray folios are also listed. References are also given to modern works containing descriptions / catalogues of this material.

Part II lists, in alphabetical order, all works other than those containing the original miniatures. They include contemporary historical and other texts, catalogues of collections and exhibitions, reference works, and secondary work on Mughal miniatures published in books or journals.

PART I

'Aja'ib al Makhluqat, CBL (*c.* 1575-1600). 16 miniatures. Catalogue: T.W. Arnold and J.V.S. Wilkinson, *The Library of A. Chester Beatty: A Catalogue of the Indian Miniatures*, London, Vol. I, pp. 26-7, pls. 50-2.

A'in-i Sikandari of Amir Khusrau, MMA, no. 13.228 (Lahore, *c.* 1595-1600). see *The Art of Islam*, cat. no. 122.

Akbarnama, VA, IS, 2-1896, no. 117 (*c.* 1602-5). 116 miniatures. Pub. sel., D. Levine and W.M. Spink, *Akbarnama: Catalogue*, New York, n.d.; G. Sen, *Paintings from the Akbarnama*, New Delhi, 1984; S.P. Verma, "Illustrated *Akbarnama* of sixteenth century Mughal School", *ROOPA*, Vol. LI (nos. 1-2), 1980.

——, CBL (*c.* 1602-5). 61 miniatures. Catalogue: Arnold and Williamson, op. cit., Vol. I, pp. 4-12, Vol. III, pls. 6-37.

——, GL (*c.* 1595-1600). 12 miniatures.

——, BM, Or. 12988 (*c.* 1604). 39 miniatures. Catalogue: N.M. Titley, *Miniatures from Persian Manuscripts*, London, 1977, pp. 4-5, no. 11. Pub. sel., F.R. Martin, *The Miniature Painting and Painters of Persia, India and Turkey*, London, 1912, Vol. II, pls. 182-3; Verma, "Aspects of Paintings in the British Museum Manuscript of the *Akbarnama*, *LALIT*, No. 27, 1993, pp. 20-9, frontispiece and pls. xi-xiii.

——, WAG. Pub., M.C. Beach, *The Grand Mogul: Imperial Mughal Painting (1600-1660)*, Williamstown, Mass., 1978, pp. 41-3, pls. on pp. 42-3.

——, IOL. Pub., T. Falk and M. Archer, *Indian Miniatures in the India Office Library*, London, 1981, p. 55, no. 22.

——, FGA. Pub., Beach, *The Imperial Image: Paintings for the Mughal Court*, Washington, D.C., 1981, 115-119.

——, CK. Pub., B.W. Robinson (ed.), *The Islamic Painting and the Arts of the Book*, London, 1976, p. 253, pl. 36.

——, KM. Pub., sel., S. Ray, *Humayun in Persia*, Calcutta, 1948, pl. 4.

——, CEB. Pub., Binney, Edwin 3rd, *Indian Miniatures from the Collection of Edwin Binney 3rd*, Portland, 1973, no. 20.

Akbarnama, London Colnaghi. Pub., Falk, "Mughal and Rajput Painting" in M. Goedhuis, *Indian Painting*, London, 1978, p. 27, pl. on p. 83.

Akbar-i Barmakiyan, Colnaghi, London (*c.* 1595). Pub. sel., Falk, op. cit., p. 24, pl. on p. 77.

Akhlaq-i Nasiri, Prince Sadruddin Aga Khan Collection, Geneva (*c.* 1600). Pub. sel., A. Welch, "Islamic Calligraphy: The Pen is the beacon of Islam", *Orientations*, Vol. 15(8), 1984, p. 18, fig. 1; M. Brand and G.D. Lowry, *Akbar's India: Art from the City of Victory*, New York, 1985, pp. 140-1, no. 19.

Anwar-i Suhaili, SOAS (dated 1570). 24 miniatures. Pub., J. Seyller, "The School of Oriental and African Studies, *Anwar-i Suhayli*: the illustrations of a De Luxe Mughal Manuscript", *AAA*, Vol. XXXVIII, 1985.

——, BM, Add. 18579 (dated 1604/11). The colophon is dated AH 1019 (AD 1610-11). But the work of illustrating this manuscript had begun much earlier. Painting no. 4 is dated AH 1013. 34 miniatures. Catalogue: Titley, op. cit., pp. 62-, no. 188. Pub., J.V.S. Wilkinson, *The Lights of Canopus: Anwar-i Suhaili*, London, 1929.

Baburnama, BM, Or. 3714 (*c.* 1598). 116 miniatures. Catalogue: C.H. Rieu, *Catalogue of the Persian Manuscripts in the British Museum*, London, 1879-95 (supp. vol., pp. 51-2); Titley, pp. 122-5, no. 268. Pub. Sel., H. Suleiman, *Miniatures of Baburnama*, Tashkent, 1970.

——, NM, no.50.326 (*c.* 1598). 144 miniatures. Pub., M.S. Randhawa, *Paintings of the Baburnama*, New Delhi, 1983.

——, SMOC (*c.* 1598). 69 miniatures. Pub. sel., S.I. Tyulayev, *Miniatures of Babur Namah*, Moscow, 1960.

——, VA (*c.* 1600). 17 miniatures.

——, BLO (Elliot 19). Mentioned: Arnold and Wilkinson, op. cit., pp. xviii.

——, MDuL (*c.* 1600). 2 miniatures. Pub., I. Stchoukine, *Les Miniatures Indiennes de l'Epoque des Grands Moghols du Musee du Louvre*, Paris, 1929, pls. 3-4.

——, BKB, no. 9069 (dated 1596-7). 25 miniatures. Pub., S.P. Verma, "Anwar-i Suahili—an illustrated manuscript of Akbar's Court in the Collection of Bharat Kala Bhavan, Varanasi", *Roopa-Lekha*, Vol. XLIV(1-2), 1977; Rai Krishnadasa, *Anwar-e-Suahili (Iyar-i-Danish)*, Varanasi, 1999.

——, FAM (*c.* 1600). I Miniature. Pub., S.C. Welch, *Art of Mughal India, Painting and Precious Objects*, New York, 1963, pl. 9.

——, WAG, W. 596 (*c.* 1600). 31 miniatures. Mentioned: J.P. Losty, *The Art of the Book in India*, London, 1982, p. 90, no. 63.

——, Colnaghi, London (*c.* 1600). 6 miniatures. Pub. sel., E. Smart, "Six folios from a dispersed manuscript of the Baburnama" in M. Goedhuis, ed. *Indian Painting*, London, 1978, pp. 109-32.

——, GMA (dated 1539 [?]). 18 miniatures. Pub. sel., R. Williams, *An Empire Builder of Sixteenth Century*, Allahabad, 1978, pls. 1-2, 11-2, 14-5.

Baharistan, BLO (Elliot MS 254), no. 963 (dated AH 983/AD 1575). 6 miniatures (*c.* 1595-1600). Catalogue: H. Ethe and E. Sachau, *Catalogue of the Persian, Turkish, Hindustani and Pushtu Manuscripts in the Bodleian Library*, Oxford, 1989, pt. 1, p. 634. Pub. sel., *Mughal Miniatures of the Earlier Periods*, Bodleian Library, Oxford, Book no. 9, Oxford, 1953, pls. 8-12.

Bostan of Sadi, CPH (*c.* 1600). Welch, op. cit., pp. 165-6, pl. 23.

——, FAM (dated AH 1009/AD 1605).

——, Collection of N. Boman Behram, Bombay (*c.* 1595).

——, BM, Add. 27262. 10 miniatures (*c.* 1630). Described: Losty, op. cit., pp. 97-8, no. 79.

——, Private Collection (formerly in Rothschild and Goelet Collection), *c.* 1600. Mentioned: Beach, *The Grand Mogul & C.*, op. cit., p. 118.

Darabnama, BM, Or. 4615 (*c.* 1588). 152 miniatures. Catalogue: Rieu, op. cit., p. 241, no. 385; Titley, pp. 8-11, no. 18.

Deval Rani Khizr Khan, NM, L.53-217 (*c.* 1567). 2 miniatures. Pub., Losty, pp. 86-7, no. 56.

Diwan of Amir Nizamuddin Hasan Dihlavi, WAG, no. W.650 (dated AH 1011/AD 1602-3). 14 miniatures. Pub. sel., R. Ettinghausen, *Paintings of Sultans and Emperors of India in American Collections*, Delhi, 1961, pl. 8; Losty, op. cit., p. 94, no. 72.

Diwan of Anwari, FAM, no.1960.117.8 (formerly in CDP), dated AH 988/AD 1580. Pub. sel., Welch, pls. 4 A-D; Welch and A. Schimmel, *Anwari's Diwan: A Pocket Book of Akbar*, New York, 1983, pls. 1-9.

Diwan-i Hafiz, RL (*c.* 1582-5). 11 miniatures. Pub. sel., Verma, "An illustrated manuscript of *Diwan-i Hafiz* of Akbar's court in the collection of Wali Ahad Rampur", *ROOPA*, Vol. L, nos. 1-2, 1978-9.
——, CBL dated AH 990/AD 1582). Catalogue: Arnold and Wilkinson, Vol. I, 78-80; Vol. III, pl. 97.
——, BM, Or. 7573 (*c.* 1610). 8 miniatures. Catalogue: Titley, p. 60, no. 167.
——, Thos. Grenville Collection (*c.* 1600) 19 miniatures. Pub. sel., Losty, p. 94, no. 73.
Diwan of Jami, Collection of Mme de Behague, France. Mentioned: Arnold and Wilkinson, p. xxvii; Asok K. Das, *Mughal Painting during Jahangir's Time*, Calcutta, 1978, p. 255, n. 10.
Diwan of Shahi, Private Collection (*c.* 1595). 2 miniatures. Welch, pls. 5A and B.
Gulistan of Sadi, RAS, no. 258 (dated 1581). 1 miniature. Pub., Sir Leigh Ashton (ed.), *The Art of India and Pakistan*, London, 1948, pl. 121.
——, BM, Or. 5302 (*c.* 1590). 13 miniatures. Catalogue: Titley, p. 147, no. 348.
——, WAG, no. 668 (*c.* 1610). Pub. sel., Ettinghausen, op. cit., pl. 10 and text.
——, BLO, no. 2585, MS. Pers. d.43 (dated AH 1050/AD 1640). 51 miniatures. Catalogue: A.F.L. Beeston, *Catalogue of the Persian, Turkish, Hindustani and Pushtu Manuscripts in the Bodleian Library*, pt. 3, Oxford, 1954, p. 31.
——, CAM, nos. 1950. 284-8 and 290; 1951.299 and 300 (*c.* 1600). 8 miniatures. Pub., E.S. Smart and D.S. Walker, *Pride of the Princes: Indian Art of the Mughal Era in the Cincinnati Art Museum*, Ohio, pp. 117-23, pls. 3a-3h.
——, Private Collection (formerly in the collection of Marquess of Bute). 6 miniatures (painted in 1644). See Welch, *Indian Art and Culture (1300-1900)*, New York, 1985, cat. no. 158.
——, Colnaghi, London, (*c.* 1600). Pub., Falk, p. 25, no. 9, pl. on p. 26.
——, CBL, MS. 22 (dated AH 1038/AD 1628-9). 9 miniatures. Pub. sel., Losty, pp. 98-9, no. 80.
Hamzanama, VMB (*c.* 1565-80). 60 miniatures. Pub., H. Gluck, *Die Indischen Miniaturen des Haemaze -Romanes* Wien, 1925, text and pls. 1-60; Erster Band, *Hamza-Nama*, Graz, 1982.
——, MMA (*c.* 1565-80). 5 miniatures.
——, BMB (*c.* 1565-80). 4 miniatures.
——, FGA (*c.* 1565-80). 3 miniatures. Pub. sel., Ettinghausen, pl. 2 and text.
——, Collection of J.F. Lewis, Philadelphia (*c.* 1570). 2 miniatures.
——, CBL (*c.* 1570). 2 miniatures. Catalogue: Arnold and Wilkinson, Vol. I, p. 11, Vol. II, pls. 1-2.
——, One miniature each in Art Institute, Chicago; FAM; CPMA; Free Library, Philadelphia; Kevorkian Foundation, New York; Collection of Bickford, Cleveland; Collection of S.M. Minkenhof, New York; BM; BKB and PWM.
Harivansha, MMA (*c.* 1590-5). Pub. sel., Welch, *Art of Mughal India & C.*, op. cit., p. 28, pl. 13.
——, SML (*c.* 1590), no. 57.106.12. 9 miniatures.
——, VA (*c.* 1590). Pub. sel., R. Skelton, "Mughal Paintings from the *Harivansh* Manuscript", *Victoria and Albert Museum Year Book*, No. 1, London, 1969.
'Iyar-i Danish, CBL (*c.* 1600). 96 miniatures. Catalogue: Arnold and Wilkinson, Vol. I, pp. 12-21, Vol. III, pls. 38-47.
——, CCJ, PWM (*c.* 1600). 52 miniatures. Catalogue: K. Khandalavala and Moti Chandra, *Miniatures and Sculptures, Collection of Sir Cowasji Jehangir*, Bombay, 1965, p. 17, pl. C.
——, IOL, no. 1403 (*c.* 1780-82, Provincial Mughal School). 35 miniatures. Catalogue: Falk and Archer, op. cit., pp. 176-80, no. 352.
Jami-ut Tawarikh, IL (dated AH 1007/AD 1598). 98 miniatures. Pub. sel., H. Knizkora, O. Kuthanova and J. Marek, *The Jenghis Khan Miniatures from the Court of Akbar the Great*, Czechoslovakia, 1963, text and pls. 1-34.
——, CJP (*c.* 1600). 2 miniatures. Pub., Binney, op. cit., p. 39, no. 17.
——, FGA, no. 53.31 (*c.* 1600).
Jog Bashisht, CBL, MS. 5 (dated AH 1012/AD 1603). 41 miniatures. Catalogue: Arnold and Wilkinson, Vol. I, pp. 21-5, Vol. II, pls. 48-9.

Khamsa of Amir Khusrau, WAG, no. W.624 (dated AH 1007 / AD 1597-8). 21 miniatures. Pub. sel., Ettinghausen, text and pl. 6; Losty, pp. 91-2, no. 66.

——, MMA (Gift of Alexander Smith Cochran), *c.* 1595-1600. Pub., sel., Welch, *Art of Mughal India & C.*, pp. 26-7, pls. 8 A and 8B.

——, PSB (*c.*1600). Mentioned: H. Goetz, "Indian Miniatures in German Museums and Private Collections", *EAQ*, Vol. 2, 1930, p. 147; Das, op. cit., p. 252.

Khamsa of Mir Ali Shir Navai, RLWC, MS.A.8. 6 miniatures (*c.* 1605). Pub. sel., Losty, p. 96, no. 77.

Khamsa of Nizami, BM, Or. 12208 (dated AH 1004 / AD 1596-7). 38 miniatures. Catalogue: Titley, pp. 142-3, no. 323. Pub. sel., Martin, op. cit., Vol. II, pls. 178-81; G. Warner, *Descriptive Catalogue of Illuminated Manuscripts in the Library of C.W. Dyson Perrins*, Oxford, 1920.

——, WAG, W. 613 (*c.* 1605). 6 miniatures. Pub., Welch, "The Emperor Akbar's *Khamsa* of Nizami", *JWAG*, 1959.

——, CK (*c.* 1585-90). 35 miniatures. Catalogue: B.W. Robinson (ed.), *Islamic Painting and the Arts of the Book (The Keir Collection)*, London, 1976, pp. 238-48, pls. 32-3, 109-16; Losty, p. 89, no. 61.

——, BNP, MS Smith-Lesouef 216 (*c.* 1551-54). 10 miniatures (miniature on folio 4 is ascribed to Maulana Darvish Muhammad). PUb., Francis Richard, "An Unpublished Manuscript from the Atelier of the Emperor Humayun, the Khamsa Smith-Lesouef 216 of the Bibliotheque Nationale" in Francoise, `Nalini' Delvoye, *Confluence of Cultures, French Contributions to Indo-Persian Studies*, New Delhi, 1994, pp. 43-50, pls. I-XII.

——, CACA (*c.* 1600). 35 miniatures.

——, AM (*c.* 1600). 2 miniatures.

——, CBL (dated AH 1022 / AD 1613). Catalogue: Arnold and Wilkinson, Vol. I, pp. 76-8, Vol. III, pl. 96.

Kathasaritsagar, CACA (*c.* 1590). 19 miniatures. Pub. sel., A.C. Ardeshir, "The Ardeshir Collection of Mughal Miniatures", *ROOPA*, Vol. I, no. 2, 1940.

——, LACM (*c.* 1590).

——, CEB (*c.* 1590). Pub., Binney, no. 26.

Kitab-i Saat, H. Kevorkian Collection (dated 1583). 12 miniatures. Pub. sel., Falk, pp. 19-22, no. 5, pls. on pp. 20-1 and 79.

——, RL (*c.* 1580-5). 157 miniatures. Pub. sel., K. Khandalavala and J. Mittal, "An early Akbari illustrated manuscript of Tilasm and Zodiac", *LALIT*, No. 14, 1961.

——, Navin Kumar Collection, New York (dated AH 991 / AD 1583), copied at Hajipur by Muhammad Yusuf for Mirza Aziz Koka. Pub. sel., M. Brand and G.D. Lowry, *Akbar's India: Art from the Mughal City of Victory*, New York, 1985, p. 150, no. 56, illustration on p. 85; M.C. Beach, *Mughal and Rajput Painting: The New Cambridge History of India*, Vol. 1:3, Cambridge, 1992, fig. 43.

Kulliyyat of Sadi, CBL (dated AH 1056 / AD 1646). 36 miniatures. Catalogue: Arnold and Wilkinson, Vol. I, pp. 72-5, no reproduction.

——, GMA (dated AH 1011 / AD 1602), MS. 206. Mentioned: Losty, p. 92, no. 67.

Laila-e Majnun of Nizami, IOL, no. 381 (dated AH 965 / AD 1557), miniatures apparently painted later (in 1600). 5 miniatures. Catalogue: H. Ethe, *Catalogue of Persian Manuscripts in the Library of the Indian Office*, Oxford, 1930; 1937, p. 605. Pub. sel., R.H. Pinder-Wilson, "Three illustrated manuscripts of the Mughal period", *AOS*, Vol. II, 1957.

——, BLO (dated AH 971 / AD 1563). 9 miniatures (*c.* 1600). Catalogue: Beeston, op. cit., p. 92. Pub. sel., *Mughal Miniatures & C.*, op. cit., pls. 1-7.

Majma'-al Gharaib, CBL (*c.* 1650-60). 86 miniatures. Catalogue: Arnold and Wilkinson, Vol. I, pp. 39-41, Vol. III, pl. 74.

Masnavi of Zafar Khan, RAS, MS. Pers. 310 (dated AH 1074 / AD 1662-3). 11 miniatures. Mentioned: Ashton, op. cit., p. 168, no. 722. Pub. sel., Losty, p. 101, no. 83; Pinder-Wilson, op. cit.

Matla' al Anwar of Amir Khusrau, MMA (Gift of Alexander Smith Cochran, no. 13.228.26), *c.* 1595-1600. 8 miniatures. Pub. sel., Ettinghausen, text and pl. 7.

Navrang-i Ishq, CBL (*c.* 1690). 11 miniatures. Catalogue: Arnold and Wilkinson, Vol. I, pp. 41-3, Vol. III, pl. 75.

Nafhat'al Uns, BM, Or. 1362 (dated AH. 1012 / AD 1602-3). 17 miniatures. Catalogue: Rieu, p. 350; Titley, p. 69, no. 207.

Padshahnama, RLWC, no. 773 (dated AH 1068 / AD 1657). 43 miniatures. Pub., M.C. Beach, Ebba Koch and W. Thackston, *King of the World: The Padshahnama, an Imperial Mughal Manuscript from the Royal Library, Windsor Castle*, London, 1997; Verma, "Seventeenth century illustrated manuscript of the *Padshahnama*", *ROOPA*, Vol. LVIII, nos. 1-2, 1986; Beach, *The Grand Mogul & C.*, op. cit., p. 85.

——, CJP (*c.* 1640). 1 miniature. Pub., Beach, *The Grand Mogul & C.*, pp. 81-4, nos. 25.

——, FGA, nos. 42.17a and 42.18a (*c.* 1660). Pub., Welch, *Imperial Mughal Painting*, London, 1978, pls. 31-2.

——, BLO, Ousely, Add. 173, no. 13 (*c.* 1600). Pub., T.W. Arnold and L. Binyon, *The Court Painters of the Grand Moghuls*, Oxford, 1921, pl. 36.

——, MG (*c.* 1650-60). Pub., J. Auboyer, *Rarities of the Musee Guimet*, New York, 1975, fig. 69.

——, CSRS (*c.* 1650-60). Pub., Anand Krishna (ed.), *Chhavi*, Banaras, 1971, pl. H.

Rajkunwar, CBL (dated AH 1013 / AD 1604). 51 miniatures. Mentioned: Das, op. cit., pp. 60-2, pls. 4-5; Losty, pp. 94-5, no. 74.

Ramayan, FGA, no. 07.271 (dated AH 1007 / AD 1598-9). 130 miniatures. Pub. sel., Ettinghausen, text and pls. 3-4; Beach, *The Grand Mogul & C.*, pp. 128-35, nos. 15a-q.

Razmnama, SMS (dated 1588). 169 miniatures. Pub., T.H. Hendley, *The Razm Namah Manuscript, Memorials of Jaypore Exhibiton*, Vol. 5, London, 1883.

——, MMA (*c.* 1600-5). 3 miniatures. Pub. sel., Ettinghausen, text and pl. 5.

——, PWM (*c.* 1600-5). 3 miniatures.

——, BM, Or. 12076 (dated AH 1007 / AD 1598). 24 miniatures. Catalogue: Titley, p. 134, no. 292.

——, VA (*c.* 1600-5). 3 miniatures. Described: Ashton, p. 147, no. 654.

——, CMA (George P. Bick Collection), no. 30965 (*c.* 1600-5).

——, SMPG, no. 198 / 1-32 (dated AH 1007 / AD 1598). 32 miniatures. Catalogue: O.C. Gangoly, *Critical Catalogue of the Indian Miniatures in the Baroda Museum*, Baroda, 1961, pp. 10-3.

——, H. Kevorkian Collection (dated 1616). Pub., Falk, p. 32, no. 17, pl. on p. 84.

——, CEB (*c.* 1616). Pub., Binney, no. 35.

——, Sir Akbar Hydari Collection, Mumbai. 12 miniatures.

——, CRBB (dated AH 1025 / AD 1616). Mentioned: M. Abdulla Chaghatai, "The illustrated edition of the *Razmnama*" *BDCRI*, Vol. 5, 1943-4.

——, IM, S.382, Reg. no.644 (*c.* 1600). Pub., Ashton, p. 143, no. 643, pl. 122.

——, FGA, no. 54.6 (*c.* 1600). Pub., Ettinghausen, text and pl.5.

——, BAAC (*c.* 1600-5). 48 miniatures. Mentioned: Chaghatai, op. cit., See alos K. Khandalavala, "A Sub-Imperial Akbari Period *Razmnama* of AD 1605" in K. Khandalavala and S. Doshi, *A Collector's Dream, Indian Art in the Collection of Basant Kumar and Saraladevi Birla and Birla Academy of Art and Culture*, Bombay, 1987, pp. 165-80.

Shahnama of Firdausi, BLO, Ouseley, Add. 175 (*c.* 1600). Pub. sel., *Mughal Miniatures & C.*, pls. 16-7.

——, CBL (*c.* 1600). 31 miniatures, 16 of Mughal origin. Catalogue: Arnold and Wilkinson, Vol. I, pp. 83-4, Vol. III, pl. 99.

——, CK, no.v. 6. See Robinson, op. cit., pp. 239-40.

——, BM, Add. 5600 (*c.* 1600). 89 miniatures. Catalogue: Rieu, Vol. II, pp. 536-7; Titley, pp. 41-2, no. 105.

——, CMDe (*c.* 1615-20).

——, State Library, Munich (*c.* 1590-1600).

Silsilah-al Dhabab, CBL (dated AH 1022 / AD 1613). 4 miniatures. Catalogue: Arnold and Wilkinson, Vol. I, pp. 39-40, Vol. III, pl. 73.

Soz-u Gudaz of Naui, BNP (*c.* 1600). Pub. sel., Goetz, *India: Five Thousand Years of Indian Art*, Bombay, 1959, p. 211.

——, BM, Or. 2839 (*c.* 1630). 3 miniatures. Pub. sel., Losty, p. 99, no. 81.

Ta'rikh-i Alfi, H.A.N. Medd. Collection, New Delhi (*c.* 1590-1600). 2 miniatures. Pub. sel., Ashton, pp. 146-7, no. 653, pl. 118.

——, BM (*c.* 1600). Pub., *BMQ*, Vol. 8, pp. 149-51.

——, CMA (*c.* 1600). Pub., BCMA, June 1932, pp. 95-7.

——, FGA (*c.* 1600).

——, CAG (*c.* 1600). Pub. sel., M. Mahfuzul Haq, "Discovery of a portion of the original manuscript of *Ta'rikh-i Alfi*, written for the Emperor Akbar", *ISC*, Vol. 5, 1931; also in *BSOS*, 1934.

Ta'rikh-i Khandan-i Timuria (also *Timurnama*), OPL (*c.* 1584-8). 132 miniatures. Catalogue: M.A. Muqtadir and E. Denison Ross, *Catalogue of the Arabic and Persian Manuscripts in the Oriental Public Library at Bankipore*, Vol. VII, Calcutta, 1921, pp. 40-48; Verma, "Miniatures of the *Tarikh-i Khandan-i Timuria*", *ROOPA*, Vol. XLIII, nos. 1-2, 1976.

Tutinama, CMA (Gift of Mrs. Dean Pery), *c.* 1570-5. Pub. sel., Welch, *Art of Mughal India and C.*, pls. 3(A-D). A. Muhammed Simsar (tr. and ed.), *The Cleveland Museum of Art's Tuti-Nama, Tales of a Parrot*, Austria, 1978, pls. 1-48; Pramod Chandra, *The Tutinama of the Cleveland Museum of Art and the Origins of Mughal Painting*, Chicago, 1976, pls. 47-61. See also Anand Krishna, "A reassessment of the *Tutinama* illustrations in the Cleveland Museum of Art (and related problems on earliest Mughal paintings and painters)", *AA*, Vol. 35(3), 1973; Verma, "Origins of the Mughal School of Painting" in *Art and Culture, Felicitation Volume in Honour of Professor S. Nurul Hasan*, A.J. Qaisar and S.P. Verma (eds.), Jaipur, 1993, pp. 60-2.

——, BKB (*c.* 1575).

——, NM (*c.* 1575).

——, CEB (*c.* 1570-5). Pub., Binney, no. 14.

——, Colnaghi, London (*c.* 1580). Pub., Falk, p. 18, no. 4, pl. on p. 78.

——, CBL, MS 21 (*c.* 1580). 103 miniatures. Pub. sel., Ashton, p. 142, no. 637, pl. 120; Losty, pp. 88-9, no. 60.

Tuzuk-i Jahangiri (or *Jahangirnama*), RL (*c.* 1620). Pub. sel., P. Brown, *Indian Painting under the Mughals,* AD *1550 to* AD *1750*, Oxford, 1924, pls. 19-20; Das, p. 135.

Zafarnama, BM, Or. 1052 (dated AH 1009 / AD 1600). 7 miniatures. Catalogue: Rieu, Vol. II, p. 176; Titley, p. 154, no. 370.

——, BLO, MS Ouseley, Add. 170 (*c.* 1600). 21 miniatures. Catalogue: Ethe and Sachau, op. cit., pp. 1088-9, no.1895. Pub. sel., *Mughal Miniatures & C.*, pl. 13.

——, BLO, MS Ouseley, Add. 167 (*c.* 1600). 37 miniatures. Catalogue: Ethe and Sachau, p. 1089, no. 1896. Pub. sel., *Mughal Miniatures & C*, pl. 22.

——, BLO, MS Ouseley, Add. 172 (*c.* 1600). 17 miniatures. Catalogue: Ethe and Sachau, p. 1091, no. 1899.

——, BLO, MS Ouseley, Add. 171 (*c.* 1600). 25 miniatures. Catalogue: Ethe and Sachau, p. 1088, no. 1894. Pub. sel., B. Gascoigne, *The Great Moghuls*, London, 1971, p. 150.

——, BLO, MS Ouseley, Add. 173 (*c.* 1590-1600). 34 miniatures. Catalogue: Ethe and Sachau, pp. 1089-90, no. 1897. Pub. sel., Gascoigne, op. cit., p. 211.

——, BLO, MS Laud, Or. 149 (*c.* 1600-5). 9 miniatures. Catalogue: Ethe and Sachau, pp. 1091-2, no. 1900. Pub. sel., *Mughal Miniatures & C.*, pls. 20-1.

——, BLO, MS Douce, Or. a.1 (*c.* 1605). 53 miniatures. Catalogue: Ethe, *Catalogue of the Persian, Turkish, Hindustani and Pushtu Manuscripts in the Bodleian Library*, Part I, Oxford, 1989, pp. 1327-8, no. 2381. Pub. sel., *Mughal Miniatures & C.*, pls. 14, 19.

——, BLO, MS Douce, Or. c.4 (*c.* 1605). 53 miniatures. Catalogue: Ethe: *Catalogue of the Persian Turkish, Hindustani and Pushtu & C.*, op. cit., pp. 1325-6, no. 2379. Pub. sel., Gascoigne, p. 137.

——, BM (Stowe Collection), Or. 16. Pub. sel., I. Stchoukine, *La Peinture Indienne a l Epoque des Grands Moghols*, Paris, 1929, pl. 21(b).

——, BM, Add. 18801. 44 miniatures. Catalogue: Titley, pp. 163-73, no. 395 (1920-9-17-013 [1-43]).

Album of Miniatures and Calligraphy, WAG. 37 miniatures. Pub. sel., Ettinghausen.

Album of Separate Miniatures of the Mughal School, CBL, 74 miniatures. Catalogue: Arnold and Wilkinson, Vol. I, pp. 57-63, Vol. III, pls. 76-93.

Album of Separate Miniatures of the Mughal School, RLWC, no. B20. 12 miniatures. See Verma, "Sixteenth century Mughal miniatures at Royal Library, Windsor and India Office Library—a survey of hitherto unnoticed miniatures", *PIHC*, Bodh Gaya, 1981; also in *ROOPA*, Vol. LVII, nos. 1-2, 1985.

Album of Separate Miniatures, Habibganj Collection, Maulana Azad Library, Aligarh Muslim University, Aligarh. Pub. sel., N.C. Mehta, *Studies in Indian Painting*, Bombay, 1926, pp. 117-9, pl. facing p. 118.

Dara Shukoh Album, IOL, 78 miniatures. Catalogue: Falk and Archer, op. cit., pp. 72-81, no. 68, pls. on pp. 379-400.

Jahangir Album, SLB. Pub. sel., E. Kuhnel and H. Goetz, *Indian Book Painting*, London, 1926.

Johnson Collection, IOL (albums 1-73). Catalogue: Falk and Archer, pp. 41-161 and pls.

Kevorkian Album, MMA. 38 miniatures. Mentioned: Beach, *The Grand Mogul & C.*, p. 76.
——, FGA. 8 miniatures. Mentioned: Beach, *The Grand Mogul & C.*, p. 76.
Album of Separate Miniatures, Sita Ram Sahu Collection, Benaras (Present whereabouts of miniatures not known). Pub. sel., Mehta, op. cit., p. 63, pl. 27.
Leningrad Album (Album of Indian and Persian Miniatures of the XVI-XVIII Centuries, HL. III miniatures. Pub. sel., A.A. Ivanova, O.F. Akimushkin, T.V. Grek and P.L.T. Gyuzalyana, *Album Indiyskikh-i Pyersidskikh Miniatyar XVI -XVIIIvv*, Moscow, 1962, Russian text with English resume, pp. 1-23 and pls.
Minto Album, CBL. 19 miniatures. Catalogue: Arnold and Wilkinson, Vol. I, pp. 27-33, Vol. III, pls. 53-65.
——, VA (nos. IM, 8-1925 to 28-1925). 21 miniatures. Pub. sel., Stchoukine, *La Peinture Indienne & C.*, op. cit., pls. 27-8, 30, 32-3, 36, 38, 40 and 44.
Muraqqa'-i Gulshan, IL. 88 miniatures. Catalogue: Badri Atabai, *Fehrist-i Muraqqat-i Kitab Khana-i Saltanati*, Tehran, Iranian Solar Year 1353. Pub. sel., H. Goetz, "The early *muraqqas* of the emperor Jahangir", *EW*, Vol. 8 (2), 1957; Y.A. Godard, "Les marges du Murakka Gulshan", *AEI*, Vol. I, 1936. Beach, "The Gulshan Album and its European sources", *BMFA*, No. 332, 1965; M. Baqir, "*Muraqqa-i Gulshan*", *JPH*, No. 5, 1957.
Nasiruddin Album, IL. Pub. sel., Godard, "Un album de portraits des princes Timurides de l Inde", *AEI*, Vol. II, 1937.
Royal Album (A) and (B), CBL 38 miniatures. Catalogue: Arnold and Wilkinson, Vol. I, pp. 27-38, Vol. III, pls. 53-72.
Wantage Album, VA. 36 miniatures. Pub. sel., C.S. Clarke, *Victoria and Albert Museum Drawings: Thirty Mogul Paintings from the school of Jahangir (17th century) and Four Panels of Calligraphy in the Wantage Bequest*, London, 1922, text and pls.

PART II

'Abdu-l Baqi Nihawandi, *Ma'asir-i Rahimi* (1616), H. Hosain (ed.), Bib. Ind. Calcutta, 1910-31. Painters noticed: Bahbud (ff. 753 a, b), Madhav (f.753b), Maulana Ibrahim *Naqqash* (f.754b), Maulana Mushfiq (f.753b), Miyan Nadim (f. 753a).
Abu'l Fazl, *Akbarnama* (1601), Ahmad Ali and Abdur Rahim (ed.), Bib. Ind., Calcutta, 1873-87, tr. H. Beveridge, RAS, Calcutta, 1897-1921.
——, *Ain-i Akbari* (1595), H. Blochmann (ed.), Bib. Ind., Calcutta, 1867-77, tr. in 3 vols., Vol.I by H. Blochmann (1868), Vols.II and III by H.S. Jarrett (1894). Revised by D.C. Phillpott (I, 1927, 1939), J. Sarkar (II and III, 1949). Painters noticed: Bihzad (I, 113), Mir Sayyid 'Ali (I, 114, 660, no.25), Khwaja 'Abdu's Samad (I, 114, 554, no.266), Muhammad Sharif (I, 582, no.351), Daswant, Basawan, Kesav, La'l, Mukund, Miskin, Farrukh Qalmaq, Madhav, Jagan, Mahesh, Khemkaran, Tara, Sanwala, Haribans, and Ram (I, 114), Amir Beg (I, 670, no.41).
Rashid Al-Tattawi, *Farhang-i Rashidi* (1653-4), Abu Tahir Zulfikar Murshidabad (ed.), RAS, Calcutta, 1872.
Adle, Chahryar, "New Data on the Dawn of Mughal Painting and Calligraphy" in Muzaffar Alam, Francoise `Nalini' Delvoye and Marc Gaborieau (eds.), *The Making of Indo-Persian Culture, Indian and French Studies*, New Delhi, 2000.
Agarwal, V.S., *Exhibition of Indian Art, Catalogue*, New Dehi, 1948.
——, (2) *Indian Miniatures (An Album)*, Delhi, 1961.
——, (3) *The Heritage of Indian Art*, New Delhi, 1964.
——, (4) *Studies in Indian Painting*, Varanasi, 1968.
Ahmad, N., "Farrukh Husain—the royal artist at the court of Ibrahim Adil Shah II", *ISC*, 30(1), 1956.
——, "The Mughal artist Farrukh Beg", *ISC*, 35, 1961.
——, "Some cultural and literary remains of emperor Humayun's visit to Iran and back to India", *INI*, 28, 1975.
Akhimushkin, O., "Painting and the art of manuscript in Iran and Western Central Asia in the sixteenth to nineteenth centuries" in C. Adle and I. Habib (eds.), *History of Civilizations of Central Asia*, Vol.V, Paris, 2003.

Alam, Ishrat, "Cotton Technology in India in the 16th century", presented at the Indian History Congress, Kurukshetra, 1982.

——, "Textile Tools as depicted in Ajanta and Mughal Paintings" in A. Roy and S.K. Bagchi (ed.), *Technology in Ancient and Medieval India*, Delhi, 1986.

——, "Diamond Mining and Trade in South India in the Seventeenth Century", *The Medieval History Journal*, New Delhi, 3, 2 (2000).

Alam, Muzaffar, Francoise 'Nalini' Delvoye and March Gaborieau, *The Making of Indo-Persian Culture, Indian and French Studies*, New Delhi, 2000.

Alfieri, B.N., "Manuhar", *EWA*, 9, 1968.

Ali, M.A., *The Apparatus of Empire: Awards of Rank, Offices and Titles to the Mughal Nobility (1574-1658)*, Delhi, 1985.

Ali, Salim, "The Mughal emperors of India as naturalists and sportsmen", *JBNHS*, 31 and 32.

Alvi, M.A. and A. Rahman (1) *Jahangir the Naturalist*, New Delhi, 1968.

Anand Krishna, *Early Mughal Painting*, New Delhi, 1971.

——, "A study of the Akbari artist: Farrukh *Chela*", *Chhavi*, Banaras, 1971.

——, (ed.), *Chhavi* (golden jubilee volume), Banaras, 1971.

——, "A reassessment of the *Tutinama* illustrations in the Cleveland Museum of Art (and related problems on earliest Mughal paintings and painters)", *AA*, 35 (3), 1973.

Archer, W.G., *Indian Painting: 15 Colour Plates*, London, 1956.

——, *Indian Painting*, New York, 1957.

——, *Central Indian Painting*, London, 1958.

——, *Indian Miniatures*, Greenwich, 1960.

——, *Romance and Poetry in Indian Painting*, London, 1965.

Archer, W.G., and Stanislaw Czuma, *Indian Art from the George P. Bickford Collection*, Cleveland, 1975.

Ardeshir, A.C., "The Ardeshir Collection of Mughal miniatures", *ROOPA*, 1(2), 1940 (notes by K. Khandalavala)

——, "Mughal miniature painting: the school of Jahangir", *ROOPA*, 2(3), 1940.

——, "Mughal miniature painting: the school of Shah Jahan", *ROOPA*, 2(4), 1940.

Arnold, Sir T.W. (1) "Some Persian and Indian miniatures", *BUM*, 31, 1917.

——, "The Johnson collection, India Office", *RUPAM*, 6, 1921.

——, *Painting in Islam*, Oxford, 1928.

——, "A note on an oriental manuscript", *IAL*, 3(2), New Series, 1929.

——, *Bihzad and His Paintings in the Zafarnama MS*, London, 1930.

——, *The Old and New Testaments in Muslim Religious Art*, London, 1932.

Arnold, Sir T.W. and L. Binyon, *The Court Painters of the Grand Moghuls*, Oxford, 1921.

Arnold, Sir T.W. and A. Grohmann, *The Islamic Book*, Munich, 1929.

Arnold, Sir T.W. and J.V.S. Wilkinson, *The Library of A. Chester Beatty: A Catalogue of the Indian Miniatures*, 3 vols., London, 1936.

——, *Chronicle of Akbar the Great (a description of a MS of the Akbarnama* illustrated by the court painters), Privately printed and circulated, 1937.

Arsdale, D.T. Van, *Islamic Art from the Collection of Edwin Binney 3rd*, Washington, 1966.

——, *The Art of Greater India (3000 BC to 1800 AD), Catalogue of the Exhibition held at Los Angeles County Museum* (March 1 to April 16, 1950), New York, 1950.

——, *The Art of Islam (Masterpieces from The Metropolitan Museum of Art, New York), Catalogue of the exhibition of Islamic art held at the Museum from 20-6-81 to 23-8-81*, New York, 1981.

Ashraf, Kunwar Muhammad, *Life and Conditions of People of Hindustan*, New Delhi, Reprint, 1970.

Ashton, Sir Leigh (ed.), *The Art of India and Pakistan: A Commemorative Catalogue of the Exhibition held at the Royal Academy of Arts, London, 1947-8*, London, 1948.

Atabai, Badri, *Fehrist-i Muraqqat-i Kitab Khana-i Saltanati*, Tehran, Shamsi, 1353 [Iranian Solar].

Atil, Esin, *The Brush of the Masters: Drawing from Iran and India*, Washington, 1978.

Auboyer, Jeannine, *Rarities of the Musee Guimet (Catalogue of an exhibition shown in the Asia House Gallery, New York, 1975)*, New York, 1975.

——, *Daily Life in Ancient India*, London, 1965.

Babur, *Baburnama* or *Tuzuk-i Baburi* (1530), Turki text, A.S. Beveridge (ed.), Leiden and London, 1905; Persian tr. by 'Abdu'r Rahim Khan-i Khanan (1590), BM, Or. 3714; tr. J. Leyden and W. Erskine, revised L. King, Oxford, 1921; and A.S. Beveridge, London, 1921; Wheeler M. Thackston, ed., tr. and annoted, New York, 1996.

Bad'auni, 'Abdul Qadir, *Muntakhabu-t Tawarikh* (1595), ed. Ahmad Ali and Lees, Bib. Ind., Calcutta, 1864-9; tr. Ranking (I, 1898), Lowe (II, 1924), Haig (III, 1925), RAS, Calcutta.

Bahrami, Mehdi, *Indian Art, Treasures from the Imperial Collections and Museums of Iran*, New York, 1949.

Bailey, Gauvin Alexander, "The Jesuits and the Grand Moghul: Renaissance Art at the Imperial Court of India, 1580-1630", *Occasional Papers*, Smithsonian Institution, Washington, D.C., 1998.

Bailey, L.H., *The Standard Encyclopedia of Horticulture*, New York, 1947.

——, *Manual of Cultivated Plants*, New York, 1966.

Bana Bhatta, *The Harsa-Carita*, tr. E.B. Cowell and F.W. Thomas, Delhi, 1961.

Band, Erster, *Hamza-Nama*, Graz, 1982.

Banerji, S.K., *Humayun Padshah*, Lucknow, 1941.

Baqir, M., "*Muraqqa-i Gulshan*", *JPH*, 5, 1957.

——, *Miniatures: Lahore Museum Collections*, 1, Lahore, 1964.

Barrett, D. and B. Gray, *Painting of India*, Lausanne, 1963.

Bayazid Bayat, *Tazkira-i Humayun-o Akbar* (1585), M. Hidayat Hosain (ed.), Bib. Ind., Calcutta, 1941.

Beach, M.C., "The Gulshan Album and its European sources", *BMFA*, 332, 1965.

——, "The Mughal Painter Kesu Das", *AAA*, 30 1976-7.

——, *The Grand Mogul: Imperial Painting in India (1600-1660)*, Williamstown, Mass, 1978.

——, "The context of Rajput painting", *AOS*, 10, 1975.

——, *The Arts of India and Nepal: The Nasli and Alice Heeramaneck Collection*, Boston, 1967.

——, "The Mughal Painter Abu'l Hasan and some English sources for his style", *JWAG*, XXXVIII, Baltimore.

——, *The Imperial Image: Paintings for the Mughal Court*, Freer Gallery of Art, Washington, D.C., 1981.

——, "An early European source in Mughal painting", *OA*, Vol. XII, No. 2, 1976.

——, "The Mughal Painter Daswanth", *AOS*, Vol. XIII, 1982.

——, *Mughal and Rajput Painting: The New Cambridge History of India*, Vol. 1:3, Cambridge, 1992.

——, Koch, Ebba and W. Thackston, *King of the World: The Padshahnama, an Imperial Mughal Manuscript from the Royal Library, Windsor Castle*, London, 1997.

Beeston, A.F.L., "The Atkinson Laila-Majnun", *Bodleian Library Records*, 4, Oxford, 1952-3.

——, *Catalogue of the Persian, Turkish, Hindustani and Pushtu Manuscripts in the Bodleian Library*, pt. 3, Oxford, 1954.

Beg, M.A.J. (ed.), *Fine Arts in Islamic Civilizations*, Kuala Lumpur, 1977.

Begley, E. Wayne, "The symbolic role of calligraphy on three Imperial Mosques of Shah Jahan", in Joanna Williams (ed.), *Kaladarsana*, New Delhi, 1981.

——, "Illustrated histories of Shah Jahan: New identifications of some dispersed paintings, and the problem of the Windsor Castle *Padshahnama*", in R. Skelton, A. Topsfield, S. Stronge and R. Crill (eds.), *Facets of Indian Art*, New Delhi, 1987.

Begley, E. Wayne and Z.A. Desai, *The Shah Jahan Nama of Inayat Khan*, New Delhi, 1990.

Bernier, Francois, *Travels in the Mughal Empire 1656-58*, tr. A. Constable, revised V.A. Smith, London, 1916.

Bhakkari, Shaikh Farid, *Zakhirat-ul Khwanin*, Syed Moinul Haq (ed.), Karachi, 1961.

Bhandari, Sujan Ra'i, *Khulasatu-i Tawarikh*, Zafar Hasan (ed.), Delhi, 1918.

Bhandarkar, D.R., "List of Inscriptions of Northern India in Brahmi and Deravative Scripts from about 200 A.C.", *Epigraphica Indica*, Vols.XIX-XXII.

Bhattacharyya, A.K., "A re-examination of the paintings of the Sultanate period", *ROOPA*, 35 (1 and 2), 1964.

Binney, Edwin 3rd., *Persian and Indian Miniatures from the Collection of Edwin Binney 3rd.*, Portland, 1962.

——, *Islamic Art from the Collection of Edwin Binney 3rd.*, Washington, D.C., 1966.

——, *Indian Miniature Paintings from the Collection of Edwin Binney 3rd. I. The Mughal and Deccan Schools with some related Sultanate Material (Exhibition catalogue: Portland Art Museum, 1 December 1973 to 20 January 1974)*, Portland, 1973.

Binyon, L., *Painting in the Far East*, London, 2nd ed., 1913.
——, *Asiatic Art, Sculpture and Paintings*, London, 1925.
——, "Indian art at Wembley: the retrospective exhibition", *RUPAM*, 21, 1925.
——, "Relation between Rajput and Moghul painting: a new document", *RUPAM*, 29, 1928.
——, "A painting of emperors and princes of the house of Timur", *BUM*, 35, 1919; revised, 54, 1929.
——, *Emperors and Princes of the House of Timur*, British Museum, London, 1930.
——, *The Spirit of Man in Asian Art*, London, 1935.
——, *Flight of the Dragon*, London, 1948.
Binyon, L., B. Gray and J.V.S. Wilkinson, *Persian Miniature Painting*, London, 1933.
Bland, David, *Book Illustration, the Illuminated Manuscript and the Printed Book*, London, 1958.
Blochet, E., *Les Enluminures des Manuscrits Orientaux de la Bibliotheque Nationale*, Paris, 1926.
——, *Musulman Painting: XII-XVII Centuries* (Eng. tr. C.M. Binyon), London, 1929.
——, "Les peintures orientales de la collection Pozzi", *Bulletin de la Societe Francaise de Reproductions de Manuscrits a Peintures*, 12, Paris, 1928.
——, "Musulman manuscripts and miniatures as illustrated in the recent exhibition at Paris", *BUM*, 2 July and 3 December, 1923.
Blunt, W., "The Mughal painters of natural history", *BUM*, 90 (539), 1948.
——, *Isfahan: Pearl of Persia*, London, 1966.
——, *Splendours of Islam*, London, 1976.
Bodleian Picture Book No.9: *Mughal Miniatures of the Earlier Periods*, Oxford, 1953.
Bonta, Robert J. Del, "Reinventing Nature: Mughal Composite Animal Painting" in S.P. Verma (ed.), *Flora and Fauna in Mughal Art*, Mumbai, 1999.
Bowie, T., *et al.*, *East-West in Art (Patterns of Cultural and Aesthetic Relationship)*, London, 1966.
Brand, Michael and G.D. Lowry, *Akbar's India: Art from the Mughal City of Victory*, New York, 1985.
Brown, Percy, *Indian Painting under the Mughals, AD 1550 to AD 1750*, Oxford, 1924.
——, *Catalogue of the Loan exhibition from the Ghose Collection of representative specimens of rare old paintings ... held at the Government School of Arts*, Calcutta, 1925.
——, "The art section of the Indian Museum, Calcutta", *IAL*, 5, New Series, 1928.
——, *Indian Painting*, Calcutta, 1953.
Brown, T.J., G.M. Meredith-Owens and D.H. Turner, "Manuscripts from the Dyson Perrins Collection", *BMQ*, 23, 1960-1.
Brunel, Francis, *Splendour of Indian Miniatures*, New York, n.d.
Bukhari, Y.K., "The manuscript of *Tuzuk-i Jahangiri* in the National Museum, New Delhi", *ISC*, 37, 1963.
Burns, Edward Mcnall, *et al.*, *World Civilization: Their History and Culture*, Vol. B, Special Indian Edition, Delhi, 1991.
Bussagli, Mario, *Indian Miniatures*, London, 1969.
Bussagli, Mario and C. Shivaramamurti, *5000 Years of the Art of India*, New York, n.d.
Butler, F. John, "The nature, influence and use of Christian art in India", *Indian Church History Review*, 8, no.1, 1974.
Campus, Arnulf, *Carmelites in Persia: A Chronicle of Carmelites in Persia and the Popal Mission of the XVII and XVIIIth Centuries*, London, 1936.
Carven, R., *Miniatures and Small Sculptures from India*, Florida, 1966.
Catalogue of the Loan Section of Indian Art, Golden Jubilee Exhibition held at Town Hall, Bombay, 20 January to 5 February 1939, Bombay, 1939.
Chaghatai, M. Abdulla, "A few Hindu miniature painters of the 18th and 19th century", *ISC*, 8, 1934.
——, *"Aqa Riza Musauvir", Md. Shafi Presentation Volume*, Lahore, 1935; also in *PIHC*, New York Graphic Society, 1938.
——, "The illustrated edition of the *Razmnama*", *BDCRI*, 5, 1943-4.
——, "Aqa Riza, Ali Riza, Riza-i Abbasi", *ISC*, 12, 1938.
——, "Mir Sayyid Ali Tabrezi", *PQ*, 5 (4), 1954.
——, "Emperor Jahangir's interviews with Gosain Jadrup and his portraits", *ISC*, 36, 1962.
Chaitanya, Krishna, *A History of Indian Painting: Manuscript, Moghul and Deccani Traditions*, New Delhi, 1979.

Chatterjee, Ratnabali, "Allegorical portraits of Asaf Khan: A study in the formation of an artistic convention", *CHJ*, 5 (2), Calcutta, 1981.
——, "European oil painting and the Mughal experience" in A. Ray, H. Sanyal and S.C. Ray (eds.), *Indian Studies*, Delhi, n.d.
Chaturbedi, Sita Ram, *Kalidas Granthavali*, Kashi, Samvat 2007.
Clarke, C.S., *Twelve Mughal Paintings of the School of Humayun*, London, 1921.
——, *Victoria and Albert Museum Drawings: Thirty Mogul Paintings from the School of Jahangir (17th century) and Four Panels of Calligraphy in the Wantage Bequest*, London, 1922.
——, "Recent accessions to the Indian section, Victoria and Albert Museum", *IAL*, 1 (2), New Series, 1927.
Cleveland Museum of Art, Handbook, Cleveland, 1978.
Codrington, K. de B., "Portraits of Akbar, the Great Mughal (1542-1605)", *BUM*, 82-3, 1943.
——, "Animals in Indian art", *GM*, 11 (5-6), 1948.
——, "Sculpture" in Leigh Ashton (ed.), *The Art of India and Pakistan: A Commemorative Catalogue of the Exhibition held at the Royal Academy of Arts, London, 1947-8*, London, 1948.
Cohn-Wiener, Ernst, "Miniatures of a Razm Nameh from Akbar's time", *IAL*, 12 (2), 1938.
——, "Miniatures from a Razm Namah", *MARG*, 11(3), 1958.
Cohn-Wiener, Ernst and J.V.S. Wilkinson, *Illustration of Indian Art*, London, 1947.
Commissariat, M.S., *Mandelslo's Travels in Western India* (AD *1638-9)*, Bombay, 1931.
Converse, Hyla S., "Selective realism and stylisation in Mughal miniatures and decorative arts" in R. Skelton, A. Topsfield, S. Stronge and R. Crill (eds.), *Facets of Indian Art*, New Delhi, 1987.
Coomaraswamy, A.K., *Selected Examples of Indian Art*, Broad Campden, 1910.
——, "Originality in Mughal painting", *JRAS*, 1910.
——, "Mughal portraiture", *OAV*, 3, 1912.
——, (tr.), *Suz-u-Gudaz* of Naui Muhammad Riza, London, 1912.
——, *The Arts and Crafts of India and Ceylon*, London, 1913.
——, *Rajput Painting*, London, 1916.
——, "Mughal paintings (schools of Akbar and Jahangir)", *BMFA*, 16(93), 1918.
——, "Portraits of Akbar, Raja Man Singh and others", *JRAS*, 1918.
——, "Portrrait of Gosain Jadrup", *JRAS*, 1919.
——, *Histoy of Indian and Indonesian Art*, London, 1927.
——, "Notes on Indian painting", *AA*, 1927.
——, "Relation of Mogul and Rajput painting", *RUPAM*, 31, 1927.
——, "Les Miniatures Orientales de la collection Goloubew au Museum of Fine Arts de Boston", *Ars Asiatica*, 13, Brussels, 1929.
——, *Catalogue of the Indian Collections in the Museum of Fine Arts, Boston, Pt. VI (Mughal Painting)*, Boston, 1930
——, *Indian Drawings*, First Series, India Society, London, 1910.
——, *Portfolio of Indian Art (Objects selected from the collection of the Museum of Fine Arts, Boston)*, Boston, 1923.
——, "Two Mughal paintings with portraits of Ali Mardan Khan", in Arthur Waley, (ed.) *Yearbook of Oriental Art and Culture (1924-5)*, London, 1925.
——, *The Transformation of Nature in Art*, New York, 1934.
Crill, Rosemary, "Court life and arts under Mughal rule" in S. Doshi (ed.), *Pageant of Indian Art*, Bombay, 1983
Crooke, W., *Tribes and Castes of the North Western Provinces and Oudh*, 4 Vols., Reprint, Delhi, 1974.
Crowe, Sylvia and Sheila Haywood, *The Gardens of Mughal India*, Delhi, 1973.
Culin, S., "Illustrations of the Romance of Amir Hamzah", *The Brooklyn Museum Quarterly*, Brooklyn, 1924.
Das, Asok K., "The Mughal royal hunt in miniature paintings", *BIM*, 2, 1967.
——, "A scene from the *Jahangirnama* in the Victoria Memorial", *BVM*, 2, 1968.
——, "The foundation of Mughal painting", *Bulletin of the Asiatic Society*, Calcutta, November 1970.
——, "Bishandas", *Chhavi* (Golden Jubilee Volume), Anand Krishna (ed.), Banaras, 1971.
——, "Ustad Mansur", *LALIT*, 17, 1974. See also Pratapaditya Pal, *Master Artists of the Imperial Mughal Court*, Bombay, 1991, pp. 39-52.
——, "Mughal Painting" in R.C. Majumdar (ed.), *History and Culture of the Indian People, VII: The Mughal Empire*, Bombay, 1974.

Das, Asok K., "Some more Mansur drawings", *LALIT*, 18, 1977.
——, "The turkey in Mughal and Amber-Jaipur paintings", *JIM*, 301, 1974 (published 1977).
——, *Mughal Painting during Jahangir's Time*, Calcutta, 1978.
——, *Treasures of Indian Painting*, Series 1, Jaipur, 1976, Series 2, Jaipur, 1978; Series 3, Jaipur 1982; Series 4, Jaipur, 1983.
——, "European elements in early Mughal painting", *BVM*, 6-7, 1972-3.
——, "Calligraphers and painters in early Mughal painting", *Chhavi*, II, Banaras.
——, "Three miniatures from the *Razmnama* of AD 1598" in A. Ray, H. Sanyal and S.C. Ray (eds.), *Indian Studies*, Delhi, n.d.
——, *Dawn of Mughal Painting*, Bombay, 1982.
——, "The Imperial *Razmnama* and *Ramayana* of the Emperor Akbar" in S. Doshi and K. Khandalavala (eds.), *An Age of Splendour—Islamic Art in India*, Bombay, 1983.
——, "An introductory note on the Emperor Akbar's *Ramayana* and its miniatures" in R. Skelton, A. Topsfield, S. Strong and R. Crill (eds.), *Facets of Indian Art*, New Delhi, 1987.
——, "The Problem of Authentic Portrait of Nur Jahan" in A.J. Qaisar and S.P. Verma (eds.), *Art and Culture, Felicitation Volume in Honour of Professor S. Nurul Hasan*, Jaipur, 1993.
——, (ed.), *Mughal Masters: Further Studies*, Mumbai, 1998.
——, "The Elephant in Mughal Painting" in S.P. Verma (ed.), *Flora and Fauna in Mughal Art*, Mumbai, 1999.
Dehejia, Vidya, "Narrative Modes in Ajanta Cave 17: A Preliminary Study", *SAS*, Vol. 7, 1991.
De Laet, *The Empire of the Great Mogol*, tr. J.S. Hoyland and S.N. Banerjee, Bombay, 1928.
Deneck, M.M., *Indian Art*, tr. A.S. Smith, London, 1967.
Desai, N. Vishakha, "Portraits, Hunts, Harems and Durbars in Courtly Paintings of Rajasthan", *Orientations*, 16 (11), 1985.
Dickinson, E.C., "The treatment of nature in Moghul paintings", *PQ*, Special Issue, August 1951.
Dickson, M.B. and S.C. Welch, *The Houghton Shahnameh*, Cambridge, Mass, 1981.
Dimand, M.S., *Indian Miniature Painting*, Milan, n.d.
——, "Three Indian paintings of the early Mughal period", *BMMA*, 23, 1928.
——, "Dated specimens of Mohammedan art in the Metropolitan Museum of Art, pt. II, Manuscripts and Miniature Paintings", *BMMA*, 1 (2), New York, 1929.
——, "Persian and Indian miniature painting", *BMMA*, 30, 1935.
——, *A Handbook of Mohammedan Art*, 2nd ed., New York, 1944.
——, "The emperor Jahangir, connoisseur of paintings", *BMMA*, 2, New Series, 1944.
——, "Several illustrations from the *Dastan-i Amir Hamza* in American collections", *AA*, 11 (1-2), 1948.
——, "Mughal painting under Akbar the Great", *BMMA*, 12, 1963.
Doshi, Saryu (eds.), *The Pageant of Indian Art* (*Festival of Indian in Great Britain*), Bombay, 1983.
Doshi, Saryu and Karl Khandalavala (eds.), *An Age of Splendour—Islamic Art in India*, Bombay, 1983.
Du Ry, J. Carl, *Art of Islam*, New York, 1972.
Dye, Joseph M. III, "Payag" in Pratapaditya Pal (ed.), *Master Artists of the Imperial Mughal Court*, Bombay, 1991.
——, *The Arts of India, Virginia Museum of Fine Arts*, New Delhi, 2001.
Earnest, C. and J.W. Watson, *Indian Miniature Painting*, Madison, 1971.
Edwards, C.C., "Relations of Shah Abbas the Great of Persia with the Mughal emperors Akbar and Jahangir", *JAOS*, 35, 1915.
Ehnbom, Daniel J. (ed.), *Indian Miniatures: The Ehrenfeld Collection*, New York, 1985.
——, "The Ehrenfeld Collection of Indian Miniatures", *Orientations*, July 1987.
Ethe, H., *Catalogue of the Persian, Turkish, Hindustani and Pushtu Manuscripts in the Bodleian Library*, pt. II, Oxford, n.d.
——, *Catalogue of Persian Manuscripts in the Library of the India Office*, Oxford, 1930; 1937.
Ethe, H. and E. Sachau, *Catalogue of the Persian, Turkish and Pushtu Manuscripts in the Bodleian Library*, pt. I, Oxford, 1989.
Ettinghausen, R., "Abd-us-Samad", *EWA*, I, 1958.
——, *Paintings of Sultans and Emperors of India in American Collections*, Delhi, 1961.
——, "The emperor's choice", *De Artibus-Opuscula*, 40, New York, 1961.

——, "New pictorial evidence of Catholic missionary activity in Mughal India (early 17th century)", *Parennitas*, Munster, 1963.
——, *Islamic Painting (Indian)*. Reprint of *The Metropolitan Museum of Art Bulletin (1978)*, New York. n.d.
——, *Islamic Art*, The Metropolitan Museum of Art, New York, n.d.
Falk, Toby, "Mughal and Rajput Painting" in M. Goedhuis (ed.), *Indian Painting (Mughal and Rajput and a Sultanate Manuscript), Catalogue of the Exhibition held at Colnaghi, London, from 5th April to 3rd May 1978*, London, 1978.
Falk, Toby, Simon Digby and Michael Goedhuis, *Paintings from Mughal India*, Colnaghi, London, n.d.
Falk, Toby and Mildred Archer, *Indian Miniatures in the India Office Library*, London, 1981.
Farooqi, Anis, *Art of India and Persia*, Delhi, 1979.
——, "Reassessment on the commencement of the Dastan-i Amir Hamzah", *ROOPA*, Vol. LXII, Nos. 1&2.
Farooque, Abul Kahir Muhammad, *Roads and Communications in Mughal India*, Delhi, 1977.
Findly, E.B. and G.D. Lowry, *From the Courts of India: Indian Miniatures in the Collection of the Worcester Art Museum*, Worcester, 1981.
Foster, William, *Early Travels in India*, 1583-1619, New Delhi, First Indian Edition, 1981.
Foster, W. (ed.), *The Embassy of Sir Thomas Roe to India 1615-1619*, London, 1899.
——, (ed.), *The English Factories in India 1608-1621*, 13 vols., Oxford, 1906-27.
——, *Letters received by the East India Company from its servants in the East*, London.
——, *Early Travels in India*, New Delhi, 1968.
Galerkina, O., "Some Characteristic of Persian Miniature Painting in the Later Part of the 16th Century", *Oriental Art*, Vol.XXI, no. 3, 1975.
Gangoly, O.C., "Portrait of Shah Abbas", *RUPAM*, 8, 1921.
——, "A portrait of Humayun", *RUPAM*, 17, 1924.
——, "A historical miniature of the Jahangir school", *RUPAM*, 33-4, 1928.
——, "On the authenticity of the feminine portaits of the Mughal school", *RUPAM*, 33-4, 1928.
——, "Mughal and Rajput miniatures", *OAZ*, 12, 1936.
——, *Critical Catalogue of the Indian Miniatures in the Baroda Museum*, Baroda, 1961.
——, "Landscape in Indian literature and art" in *Radha Kumud Mookherjee Foundation Lectures, University of Lucknow, 1954 (2)*, Lucknow, 1963.
Gascoigne, B., *The Great Moghuls*, London, 1971.
Gaur, Albertine, *Women in India*, British Library, London, 1980.
Ghoshal, U.N., *Studies in Indian History and Culture*, Bombay, 1957.
Gladstone-Solomon, W.E., "Colour and the Mughals", *ISC*, 13, 1929.
——, "Jahangir and his Artists", *ISC* 3 (1), 1929.
——, "Masterpieces of Moghul painting, a critical study", *ISC*, 4, 1930.
——, "Perspective and the Moghuls", *ISC*, 5, 1931.
——, *Masterpieces of Mughal Art*, Oxford, 1933.
——, "Mughal pictures in London, Mr Y. Dawud's Collection", *ISC*, 12, 1938.
Gluck, H., *Die Indischen Miniaturen der Berliner Museum*, Cicerone, 1923.
——, *Die Indischen Miniaturen des Haemzae-Romanes*, Wien, 1925.
Gluck, H. and E. Diez, *Die Kunst Des Islam*, Berlin, n.d.
Glynn, Catherine, "An early Mughal landscape painting and related work", *BLACM*, 22(2), 1947.
Godard, Y.A., "Les marges du Murakka' Gulshan", *AEI*, I, 1936.
——, "Un album de portraits des princes Timurides de l'Inde", *AEI*, II, 1937.
Godard, Y.A. and B. Gray, *Iran -Persian Miniatures, Imperial Library*, New York, 1956.
Godden, R., *Gulbadan (Portrait of the Rose Princes)*, New York, 1980.
Goedhuis, Michael, (ed.) *Indian Painting (Mughal and Rajput and a Sultanate Manuscript)*, Colnaghi, London, 1978.
Goetz, H., "Die indischen Miniaturen der Sammlung William Rothenstein, London", *Jahrbuch der Asiatischen Kunst*, Leipzig, 1925.
——, "Indian miniatures in German museums and private collections", *EAQ*, 2, 1930.
——, *Geschichte der Indischen Miniaturmalerei*, Berlin, 1934.

Goetz, H., "Notes on Indian painting", *BBSM*, 7, 1945-50.
——, "Indian painting in the Muslim period—a revised historical outline", *JISOA*, 15, London, 1947.
——, "The problem of the origin of two medieval Indo-Persian miniatures", *ISC*, 29, 1955.
——, "The early *muraqqa's* of the Mughal emperor Jahangir", *EW*, 8 (2), 1957.
——, "The early *muraqqa's* of the emperor Jahangir", *MARG*, 11 (4), 1958.
——, "Life and art in the Mughal period, the mental background of Mughal painting and its reflection in art", *JUB*, 1958.
——, *India: Five Thousand Years of Indian Art*, Bombay, 1959.
——, *Handbook of the Collections, Baroda Museum and Picture Gallery*, Baroda, 8, 1950-2.
——, *Bilderatlas zur Kulturgeschichte Indiens in der Grossmoghul-Zeit*, Berlin, n.d.
——, *The Indian and Persian Miniature Paintings in the Rijksprentenkabinet, Amsterdam*, Amsterdam, 1958.
Goetz, H. and Mulk Raj Anand, *Indische Miniaturen*, Dresden, 1967.
Goldie, Francis, *First Christian Missions to the Great Mogul*, London, 1987.
Goswamy, B.N., *The Essence of Indian Art*, San Francisco, 1986.
——, "Coming to terms with Time Aspects of Narrative Visual Arts" in Joythidra Jain (ed.), *Picture Showmen Insights into the Narrative Tradition in Indian Art*, Mumbai, 1998.
Goswamy, B.N., and A. Dahmen-Dallapicola, *An Early Document of Indian Art, the Chitralaksana of Nagnajit*, New Delhi, 1976.
Goswamy, B.N. and Eberhard Fisher, *Pahari Painters, Court Painters of Northern India*, New Delhi, 1997.
Gradmann, E., *Miniatures Indiennes*, Lausanne, 1953.
Gray, B., "An early Mughal illuminated page", *BMQ*, 8, 1933-4.
——, "A collection of Indian portraits", *BMQ*, 10, 1955-6.
——, "Mughal miniatures from the court of Akbar", *OAZ*, 11, 1935.
——, "The art of India and Pakistan with special reference to the exhibition at the Royal Academy", *IAL*, 1947.
——, "Islamic art at the exhibition of the Royal Academy, London, November 1947 to February 1948", *AIS*, 15-6, 1951.
——, "Painting", in Leigh Ashton (ed.), *The Art of India and Pakistan: A Commemorative Catalogue of the Exhibition held at the Royal Academy of Arts, London, 1947-8*, London, 1948.
——, *Treasures of Indian Miniatures in the Bikaner Palace Collection*, Oxford, 1955.
——, *Persian Painting*, Lausanne, 1961.
——, (ed.), *The Arts of India*, New York, 1981.
Gray, B., and J.V.S. Wilkinson, "Indian paintings in a Persian museum", *BUM*, 66, 1935.
——, "Mughal miniatures from the period of Akbar", *OAZ*, 11, 1935.
Grousset, R., *The Civilization of the East: India*, New York, 1931.
——, "The great periods of Indian art illustrated in recent acquisitions of the Musee Guimet", *AAL*, 1, New Series, London, 1927.
Grube, E.J., *Islamic Paintings from the 11th to the 18th Century from the collection of Hans P. Kraus*, New York, n.d.
——, *The World of Islam*, New York, 1967.
——, *Muslim Miniature Paintings from the XIII to XIX Century from Collections in the United States and Canada*, Venezia, 1962.
Gulbadan, *Humayun-nama* (1555), tr. A.S. Beveridge, *RAS*, London, 1902, reprint 1972.
Gupta, S.N., *Catalogue of Paintings in the Central Museum, Lahore*, Lahore, 1922.
Habib, Irfan, *The Agrarian System of Mughal India (1556-1707)*, Delhi, 1963.
——, "Technological Changes and Society (13th and 14th Centuries)", *Proceedings of the Indian History Congress*, Varanasi, 1969.
——, "Changes in Technology in Medieval India", *Studies in History*, Vol. II, No. 1, New Delhi, 1980.
——, "The Technology and Economy of Mughal India", *The Indian Economic and Social History Review*, Vol. XVII, No. 1, 1980.
——, *An Atlas of the Mughal Empire*, Delhi, 1982.
——, "Exploring Medieval Gender History", *Symposia Papers: 23*, Indian History Congress, Calicut, 2000.
Hajek, Lubor, *Indian Miniatures of the Mughal School*, London, 1960.
——, *Miniatures from the East*, London, 1960.

Hallade, Madeleine, *The Gandhara Style and the Evolution of Buddhist Art*, London, 1968.
Hambly, G., *Cities of Mughal India (Delhi, Agra and Fatehpur Sikri)*, Delhi, 1968.
Haq, M. Mahfuzul, "Dara Shikoh and the fine arts of painting and calligraphy", *Muslim Review*, 2(3), 1928.
——, "The Khan-i Khanan and his painters", *ISC*, 5, 1931.
——, "Discovery of a portion of the original manuscript of *Tarikh-i Alfi*, written for the emperor Akbar", *ISC*, 5, 1931; also in *BSOS*, 1934.
Haque, Zulekha, *Terracotta Decorations of Late Medieval Bengal, Portrayal of a Society*, Dacca, 1980.
Hasan, S.M., "The Mughal school of zoological portraiture", *Arts and Letters*, Liechtenstein, 37, 1963.
Havell, E.B., *Indian Sculpture and Painting*, London, 1908.
——, *A Handbook of Indian Art*, London, 1929.
——, *The Art Heritage of India*, Bombay, 1964.
Hendley, T.H., *The Razm Namah Manuscript, Memorials of Jaypore Exhibition*, 5, London, 1883.
——, "Indian animals, true and false, in art, religion, etc.", *JIAI*, 16 (126), 1914.
——, "War in Indian art", *JIAI*, 1916.
——, "Sport in Indian art", *JIAI*, 17, 1916.
Hidayat, A. (1) "Shah Jahan", *MARG*, 11 (4), 1958.
Hodge, Sotheby and Wilkinson, *Sale Catalogue of March 1922 (MS of Naui's Suz-u Gudaz with 8 miniatures painted by Muhammad Yusuf, AH 1068 (AD 1657).*
Hosten, H.S., "European art at the Mughal court", *JUPHS*, 3, 1922.
Husain, J., *Glimpses of Medieval Indian Culture*, London, 1959.
Inerney, Terence Mc, "Manohar" in Pratapaditya Pal (ed.), *Master Artists of the Imperial Mughal Court*, Bombay, 1991.
Irwin, J., "The Heritage of Art in India: (3) the Mughal Painting", *Studio*, no. 135, 1948.
Iskandar-Beg Munshi, *Ta'rikh-i 'Alam-ara-yi 'Abbasi* (History of Shah Abbas and his predecessors), Tehran, AH 1314 (AD 1896), trans. T. Arnold.
Islam, Riazul, *Indo-Persian Relations—A Study of the Political and Diplomatic Relations between the Mughal Empire and Iran*, Lahore, 1970.
Ivanova, A.A., O.F. Akimushkin, T.V. Grek, and P.L.T. Gyuzalyana, *Al'bom Indiyskikh-i Pyersidskikh Miniatyar XVI-XVIIIvv*, Moscow, 1962, Russian text with English resume.
Jahangir, *Tuzuk-i Jahangiri* (1624), ed. S. Ahmad, Ghazipur and Aligarh, 1863-4; tr. A. Rogers, ed. H. Beveridge, London, 1904-14; Thackston, M. Wheeler (ed. and tr.), *The Jahangirnama*, New York, 1999.
Jauhar, *Tezkereh al Vakiat*, tr., Stewart, *Private Memoirs of the Mughal Emperor Humayun*, London, 1832.
Joannes, De Laet, *Empire of the Great Mogol*, tr. J.S. Hoyland, annotated by S.N. Banerjee, Bombay, 1928.
Johnson, B.B. "A preliminary study of the technique of Indian miniature painting", in Pratapaditya Pal (ed.), *Aspects of Indian Art*, Leiden, 1972.
Jones, D. (ed.), *A Mirror of Princes: The Mughals and the Medici*, Bombay, 1987.
Kalyan Krishna, "Problem of a portrait of Jahangir in the Musee Guimet, Paris, in Anand Krishna (ed.), *Chhavi*, Banaras, 1971.
Khan, Ahmad Nabi, "An illustrated *Akbarnama* manuscript in the Victoria and Albert Museum", *EW*, 19 (3-4), September-December 1969.
Khandalavala, K., *Indian Sculpture and Painting: An Introductory Study*, Bombay, 1938.
——, "Some problems of Mughal painting", *LALIT*, 11, 1965.
——, "The Mughal School and its Ramifications" in *The Development of Style in Indian Painting*, Delhi, 1974.
——, *Islamic Heritage of India*, Delhi, 1981.
——, "The Heritage of Islamic art in India" in Saryu Doshi and Karl Khandalavala (eds.), *An Age of Splendour—Islamic Art in India*, Bombay, 1983.
——, "A sub-imperial Akbari period *Razm Nama* of AD 1605" in K. Khandalavala and S. Doshi, *A Collector's Dream, Indian Art in the Collection of Basant Kumar and Saraladevi Birla and Birla Academy of Art and Culture*, Bombay, 1987.
Khandalavala, K. and Jagdish Mittal, "An early Akbari illustrated manuscript of Tilasm and Zodiac", *LALIT*, 14, 1961.

Khandalavala, K. and Moti Chandra, *Miniatures and Sculptures, Collection of Sir Cowasji Jehangir*, Bombay, 1965.
——, *New Documents of Indian Painting—A Reappraisal*, Bombay, 1970.
Khandalavala, K., Moti Chandra and Pramod Chandra, *Miniature Painting (Catalogue of the exhibition of Sir Motichand Khajanchi Collection held at Lalit Kala Academi, 1960)*, New Delhi, 1960.
Khan Iqtidar Alam, "The Coming of Gunpowder and the Response of Indian Polity" presented at Centre for Studies in Social Sciences, Calcutta, September, 1980.
——, (ed.), *Akbar and His Age*, New Delhi, 1999.
Knizkova, H., "Notes on the portrait of Ibrahim Adil Shah II of Bijapur in the Naprstek Museum, Prague" in R. Skelton, A. Topsfield, S. Stronge and R. Crill (ed.), *Facets of Indian Art*, New Delhi, 1987.
Knizkova, H., O. Kuthanova and J. Marek, *The Jenghis Khan Miniatures from the Court of Akbar the Great*, Czechoslovakia, 1963.
Koch, Ebba, "The influence of the Jesuit Mission on symbolic representations of the Mughal Emperors", *Islam in India, Studies and Commentaries*, I, 1982.
——, "The baluster column—a European motif in Mughal architecture and its meaning", *Journal of the Warburg and Courtland Institute*, 45, London, 1982.
——, "Jahangir and the angels: recently discovered wall paintings under European influence in the fort of Lahore", *South Asian Studies*, 15, New Delhi, 1983.
——, "*Pietra dura* and other artistic contacts between the Court of the Mughals and that of the Medici", in D. Jones (ed.), *A Mirror of Princes: The Mughals and the Medici*, Bombay, 1987.
——, *Mughal Art and Imperial Ideology, Collected Essays*, New Delhi, 2001.
Koshambi, Damodar Dharmanand, *An Introduction to the study of Indian History*, Bombay, 1975.
Kramrisch, Stella, *A Survey of Painting in the Deccan*, London, 1937.
——, *Painted Delight: Indian Paintings from Philadelphia Collections*, Philadelphia.
Krishnadasa, Rai, *Anwar-e-Suhaili (Iyar-i-Danish)*, Varanasi, 1999.
Krishnadasa, Rai and Humayun Kabir, *Mughal Miniatures*, New Delhi, 1955.
Krishna, Vijay, "Shaikh Phul: A Jahangiri Painting", *JISOA*, XI, 1980.
Kuhnel, Ernst, *Islamische Miniaturmalerei*, Berlin, 1922.
——, *Miniaturmalerei in Islamischen Orient*, Berlin, 1922.
——, *Moghul Malerei*, Berlin, n.d.
——, *Indische Miniaturen* (Indian miniatures in the possession of the Berlin State Museum), Berlin, n.d.
——, *Islamic Art and Architecture*, tr. Katherine Watson, London, 1962.
——, "Die Indischen Miniaturen der Sammlung Otto Sohn-Rethel", *Pantheon*, 8, 1931.
——, "History of miniature painting and drawing" in Arthur Upham Pope and Phyltes Ackerman (eds.), *A Survey of Persian Art*, V., London, 1958; reissued Tehran, London, Tokyo, 1964.
Kuhnel, Ernst and H. Goetz, *INdische Buchmalereien aus dem Jahangir-album der Staatsbibliothek zu Berlin*, Berlin, 1923; English edition, (2) *Indian Book Painting*, London, 1926.
Kwandamir, *Qanun-i Humayuni* (1534 AD), tr. Prasad, Beni, Calcutta, 1940.
Lahori, Abdul Hamid, *Padshahnama* or *Badshahnama* (1654-5), ed. Kabiruddin Ahmad and Abdur Rahim, Bib. Ind. Calcutta, 1867-72.
Lahori, Salih Kanbu, *Amal-i Salih*, text, G. Yazdani (ed.), Bib. Ind., Calcutta, 1912-46.
Lawrence, G., *L'Art Des Indes, Miniatures Moghules* Paris, 1963; English edition, *Indian Art, Mughal Miniatures*, London, 1963.
Leach, Linda York, "Painting", in Saryu Doshi (ed.), *Pageant of Indian Art, Festival of India in Great Britain*, Bombay, 1983.
——, "Catalogue of the Indian Miniatures in the Cleveland Museum of Art" (Ph.D. Thesis), Department of Art History, CASE Western Reserve University, Spring 1978.
——, "Life at Court" in *The Image of Man: The Indian Perception of the Universe through 2000 years of Painting and Sculpture*, Delhi, 1982.
——, "Painting in Kashmir from 1600-1650" in R. Skelton, A. Topsfield, S. Stronge and R. Crill (eds.), *Facets of Indian Art*, New Delhi, 1987.
Lee, S., *A History of Far Eastern Art*, London, 1964.
Lee, S. and Pramod Chandra, "A newly discovered *Tutinama* and the continuity of the Indian tradition of manuscript painting", *BUM*, 1963.

Levine, D. and W.M. Spink, *Akbarnama: Catalogue*, New York, n.d.
Lewis, Bernard (ed.), *The World of Islam*, London, 1976.
Losty, J.P., *The Art of the Book in India (Catalogue of an Exhibition Mounted at the British Library from 16 April-1 August 1982)*, British Library, London, 1982.
——, "The art of the book in India" in S. Doshi (ed.), *The Pageant of Indian Art*, Bombay, 1983.
Lugs, Jaroslay, *Fire Arms, Past and Present*, London, 1975.
Macaulay, D., "Mughal Art", *BUM*, 46, 1925.
Maclagan, E.D., *The Jesuits and the Great Mogul*, London, 1932.
——, "Mogul paintings on Christian subjects", *MW*, 23, 1933.
Makhdoomee, M. Akram, "Mechanical Artillery in Medieval India", *Journal of Indian History*, Vol. XV, Pt. 2, 1936.
Malcolm, Sir John, *A Memoir of Central India including Malwa*, 2 vols., London, 1824.
Manrique, Fray Sabastien, *Travels of Fray Sabastien Manrique 1629-1643* by C.K. Eckford Luard, Oxford, 1927.
Manucci, Niccolao, *Storia do Mogor, 1656-1712*, tr. W. Irvine, Indian Text Series, Government of India, London, 1907-8.
Marteau, G. and H. Vever, *Miniatures Persanes exposees au Musee des Arts Decoratifs*, Paris, 1912.
Martin, F.R., *The Miniature Painting and Painters of Persia, India and Turkey*, London, 1912.
——, *Miniatures from the period of Timur in a MS of the poems of Sultan Ahmad Jalair*, Vienna, 1926.
Marshall, Sir John, Alfred Foucher and N.G. Majumdar, *The Monuments of Sanchi*, Reprint, Delhi, 1982.
Mehta, N.C., "Red lilies, a newly discovered Mansur", *RUPAM*, 1920, 1924.
——, "A new picture by Bishandas", *RUPAM*, 24, 1925.
——, *Studies in Indian Painting*, Bombay, 1926.
Melikian-Chirvani, A.S., "Mir Sayeed 'Ali: Painter of the Past and Pioneer of the Future" in A.K. Das (ed.), *Mughal Masters, Further Studies*, Mumbai, 1998.
Meredith-Owens, G.M., "A new illustrated manuscript of the "*Ajab al-Makhluqat*", *BMQ*, 23, 1960-1.
——, "The British Museum manuscript of the Akbarnamah", *BUM*, 109, 1967.
Michell, George (ed.), *In the Image of Man (The Indian Perception of the Universe through 2000 Years of Painting and Sculpture)*, Catalogue of the Festival of India, held at the Hayward Gallery, London, (25 March-13 June 1982), New Delhi, 1982.
Migeon, G., *Musulman Art in the Louvre Museum*, Paris, 1922.
——, *Arts Musulmans*, Paris, 1926.
Minorsky, T. (tr.), *Calligraphers and Painters* [*A treatise by Qazi Ahmad son of Mir Munshi, circa AH 1015 (AD 1606)*], Washington, 1959.
Misra, Rekha, *Women in Mughal India (1526-1748 AD)*, Delhi, 1967.
Monserrate, S.J., *The Commentary of Father Monserrate, S.J. on his journey to the court of Akbar*, tr. J.S. Hoyland, annotated by S.N. Banerjee, London, 1922.
Moosvi, Shireen, *The Economy of Mughal Empire, c. 1595—A Statistical Study*, New Delhi, 1987.
——, "Work and Gender in Pre-Colonial India", *Socio-Economic consequences of sex-ratios in historical perspective, 1500-1900*, ed. Universita Beeoni, Milan, 1994.
——, "Society, Part II, India", *History of Civilizations of Central Asia*, Vol. V, Chahryar Adle and Irfan Habib (eds.), co-editor: Karl M: Baipakoo, Paris, 2003.
——, "Domestic Service in Pre-colonial India, Bondage, Caste and Market", *Domestic Service and the Formation of European Identity Understanding the Globalization of Domestic Work, 16th-21st Centuries*, ed. Antoinette Fauve-Chamoux, Bern, 2004.
Moreland, W.H., *India at the Death of Akbar*, Delhi, 1920.
Morris, Rekha, "Some additions to the known corpus of paintings by the Mughal artist Farrukh Chela", *AOS*, 13, 1982.
Moti Chandra, "An illustrated MS of Nal Daman in the Prince of Wales Museum, Bombay", *ROOPA*, 3, 1946
——, *The Technique of Mughal Painting*, Lucknow, 1946.
——, "Portraits of Ibrahim Adil Shah I", *MARG*, 5(1), 1951.
——, *Indian Art*, Prince of Wales Museum, Bombay, 1964.
——, *A Handbook of the Indian Art: Collection in the Prince of Wales Museum of Western India, Bombay*, Bombay, n.d.

Mulk Raj Anand, "The background of early Mughal painting", *MARG*, 11(3), 1958.
——, "Jahangir the epicurean", *MARG*, 11(4), 1958.
——, *Album of Indian Paintings*, New Delhi, 1973.
Mundy, Peter, *The Travels of Peter Mundy in Europe and Asia*, Vol.II, *Travels in Asia*, R.C. Temple (ed.), Hakluyt Society, 2nd Series, No.XXXV, London, 1914.
Muqtadir, M.A., "Note on a unique history of Timur, illustrated by the court painters of Akbar", *JBORS*, 3(2), 1917.
Muqtadir, M.A. and E. Denison Ross, *Catalogue of the Arabic and Persian Manuscripts in the Oriental Public Library at Bankipore*, Vol. VII, Calcutta, 1921.
Mustafa, Khursheed, "Travels in Mughal India", *Medieval India Quarterly*, Vol. III, nos. 3&4, New Delhi, 1958.
Mu'tamad Khan, *Iqbalnama-i Jahangiri*, Vols. I and II: ed. Naval Kishor, Lucknow, 1865; Vol. III: ed. Abdul Hai and Ahmad Ali, Bib. Ind., Calcutta, 1865.
Mutribi, *Khatirat-i Mutribi Samarqandi*, Abdul Ghani Mirzoyef (ed.), Karachi, 1977.
Nalini Delvoye, Francoise (ed.), *Confluence of Culture, French contribution to Indo-Persian Studies*, New Delhi, 1994
Nath, Narindar and K. Khandalawala, "Illustrated Islamic Manuscripts" in S.K. Doshi and K. Khandalavala (1) (eds.), *An Age of Splendour—Islamic Art in India*, Bombay, 1983.
Naqvi, S.A. Zafar, "Libraries during the Muslim rule in India", *ISC*, 19, 1945.
Nizamuddin Ahmad, *Tabaqat-i Akbari* (1592-3), ed. B. De and M.H. Hosain, Bib. Ind., Calcutta, 1913-41; tr. B. De, Bib. Ind., Calcutta, 1927
Oaten, Edward Farley, *European Travellers in India*, Lucknow, 1974.
O'Connor, V. Scott, *An Eastern Library (illustrated account of the Khuda Bakhsh Library at Bankipore)*, Glasgow, 1920
Okada, Amina, "Cinq dessins de Basawan au Musee Guimet", *AAS*, XLI, Paris 1986.
——, *Imperial Mughal Painters, Indian Miniatures from the Sixteenth and Seventeenth Centuries*, Flammarion, Paris, 1992.
Okada, Amina, and Richard Francis, *A la cour du Grand Moghul*, Paris, 1986.
——, *Oriental Miniatures and Illuminations*, Maggs Brothers, Ltd., London (i) Bulletin 11 (3), May 1967; (ii) Bulletin 20(2), March 1972; (iii) Bulletin 22(1), March 1974.
Oman, John Campbell, *Cults, Customs and Superstitions of India*, Delhi, 1972.
——, *The Mystics, Ascetics and Saints*, London, 1905.
Pal, Pratapaditya, "The enduring charm of Indian painting and Indian art from the Paul Walter Collection", *Allen Memorial Art Museum Bulletin*, 28(2), 1971.
——, (ed.), *Aspects of Indian Art*, Leiden, 1972.
——, (ed.), *Islamic Art: The Nasli M. Heeramaneck Collection*, Los Angeles, 1973.
——, *Court Paintings of India, 16th-19th Centuries*, New York, 1983.
——, (ed.), *Master Artists of the Imperial Mughal Court*, Bombay, 1991.
——, *Indian Painting: A Catalogue of the Los Angeles County Museum of Art Collection*, Vol. I (1000-1700), California, 1993.
——, *et al.*, *Romance of the Taj Mahal*, New Delhi, 1989.
Panigrahi, Krishna Chandra, *Archaeological Remains at Bhubaneswar*, New Delhi, 1961.
Parihar, Subhash, *Land Transport in Mughal India: Agra-Lahore Mughal Highway and its Architectural Remains*, New Delhi, 2008.
Payne, C.H., *Akbar and the Jesuits*, London, 1926.
——, *Jahangir and the Jesuits*, London, 1930.
Pelsaert, Françisco, "*Remonstrantie*" (1626), tr. W. Moreland and Geyl as *Jahangir's India*, Cambridge, 1925, reprint, Delhi, 1972.
Pinder-Wilson, R.H., "Three illustrated manuscripts of the Mughal period", *AOS*, 2, 1957.
——, "A Persian translation of the *Mahabharata*: a note on the miniatures", *BMQ*, 20(1), 1956.
——, *Paintings from the Muslim Courts of India (Catalogue of the exhibition of the World of Islam Festival, 1976)*, held at Prints and Drawings Gallery, British Museum, from 13th April to 11th July 1976, London, 1976.
——, (ed.), *Paintings from Islamic Lands*, Oxford, 1969.

Polunin, Oleg and Adam Stainton, *Flowers of the Himalaya*, Delhi, 1984.

Pope, Arthur Upham and Phyltes Ackerman (eds.), *A Survey of Persian Art from Prehistoric Times to the Present*, first ed. 1938-9; reissued, Tehran, London, Tokyo, 1964.

Possehl, G.L., *The Indus Civilization: A Contemporary Perspective*, New Delhi, 2002.

Pramod Chandra, "Ustad Salivahana and the development of popular Mughal art", *LALIT*, 8, 1960.

——, "Mughal portraiture", *TIA*, 1962.

——, *The Tutinama of the Cleveland Museum of Art and the Origins of Mughal Painting*, Chicago, 1976.

Pramod Chandra and Daniel J. Ehnbom, *The Cleveland Tutinama Manuscript and the Origins of Mughal Painting*, Chicago, 1973.

Prasad, Pushpa, "Jahangir and Jains", *ISC*, Vol. LVI, No. 1, 1982.

Princely Paintings from Mughal India (catalogue of the loan exhibition of Mughal painting, Bradford, 1980), British Museum, London, 1980.

Purchas, Samuel, *Purchas: His Pilgrimes*, Vol. X, London, MCMV.

Qaisar Ahsan Jan, "Ship-building in the Mughal Empire during the Seventeenth Century" *The Indian Economic and Social History Review*, Vol. V, No. 2, 1968.

——, *Building Construction in Mughal India: The Evidence from Painting*, New Delhi, 1988.

——, "Agricultural Technology depicted in Mughal Painting", *Itinerario*, Vol. XVI, No. 2, Leiden, 1992.

Qaisar Ahsan Jan and S.P. Verma (eds.), *Art and Culture, Felicitation Volume in Honour of Professor S. Nurul Hasan*, Jaipur, 1993.

——, and S.P. Verma (eds.), *Art and Culture, Endeavours in Interpretation*, New Delhi, 1996.

——, and S.P. Verma (eds.), *Art and Culture, Painting and Perspective*, New Delhi, 2002.

Qandhari Haji Muhammad 'Arif, *Ta'rikh-i Akbari* (1580), Imtiyaz Ali Arshi (ed.), Rampur, 1962.

Qazi Ahmad, *Calligraphers and Painters* (dated AH 1015 / (AD 1606), tr. into Russian from the Persian text by V. Minorsky with an introduction by B.N. Jabhoder; tr. from Russian text into English by T. Minorsky, Washington, 1959.

Qazwini, Mulla 'Alaud-Daula, *Nafa'is-al Ma'asir*, MAL, MS, dated 1573, Aligarh Muslim University.

Ramaswamy, Vijya, "Aspects of Women and Work in Early South India" in Kumkum Roy (ed.), *Women in Early Indian Societies*, New Delhi, 1999.

Randhawa, M.S., *Kangra Paintings of the Bhagawata Purana*, New Delhi, 1960.

——, *Indian Miniature Painting*, New Delhi, 1981.

——, *Paintings of the Baburnama*, National Museum, New Delhi, 1983.

Randhawa, M.S. and J.K. Galbraith, *Indian Painting, the Scene, Themes and Legends*, Boston, 1968.

Rashid, A., *Society and Culture in Medieval India (1206-1556 AD)*, Calcutta, 1965.

Rawlinson, H.G. *et al.*, *Indian Art*, London, 1947.

Rawson, Philip S., *Indian Painting*, London, 1961.

Ray, Acharya P. Chandra, *History of Chemistry in Ancient and Medieval India*, Calcutta, 1956.

Ray, Niharranjan, *Mughal Court Painting*, Calcutta, 1975.

Ray, Sukumar, *Humayun in Persia*, Calcutta, 1948.

Rice, David Talbot, *Islamic Art*, Thames and Hudson, 1965.

——, *Islamic Painting—A Survey*, Edinburgh, 1971.

Richard, Francis, "An unpublished Manuscript from the Atelier of Emperor Humayun, the *Khamsa* Smith-Lesouef 216 of the Bibliotheque Nationale" in Francoise `Nalini' Delvoye (ed.), *Confluence of Culture, French Contributions to Indo-Persian Studies*, New Delhi, 1994.

Rich, Vivian A., "Mughal Floral Painting and its European Sources", *OA*, New Series, XXXIII(2), 1987.

Ridley, M., *Oriental Art, India, Nepal and Tibet for Pleasure and Investment*, London, 1970.

Rieu, C.H., *Catalogue of the Persian Manuscripts in the British Museum*, London, 1879-95.

Rizvi, Saiyid Athar Abbas, *Religious and Intellectual History of the Muslims in Akbar's Reign (1556-1605)*, New Delhi, 1975.

——, *A History of Sufism in India*, Delhi, 1983.

Robinson, B.W., *The Kevorkian Collection: Islamic and Indian MSS., Miniature Paintings and Drawings*, New York, 1953.

——, *A Descriptive Catalogue of the Persian Paintings in the Bodleian Library*, Oxford, 1958.

Robinson, B.W., "Shah Abbas and the Mughal ambassador Khan Alam: the pictorial record", *BUM*, February 1972.
——, (ed.), *Islamic Painting and the Arts of the Book (The Keir Collection)*, London, 1976.
——, *Persian Miniatures in the India Office Library*, London, 1976.
——, (ed.), *Persian and Mughal Art (Catalogue of the Exhibition of Persian and Mughal Art held at Colnaghi, London from 7th April to 22nd May 1976)*, London, 1976.
——, *Persian Paintings in the John Rylands Library*, London, 1980.
Roe, Thomas and John Fryer, *Travels in India in the Seventeenth Century*, New Delhi, 1993.
Rogers, J.M., *Mughal Miniatures*, London, 1993.
Roy, A. and S.K. Bagchi (ed.), *Technology in Ancient and Medieval India*, Delhi, 1986.
Roy, Kumkum (ed.), *Women in Early Indian Societies*, New Delhi, 1999.
Saqi Musta'id Khan, *Ma'asir-i 'Alamgiri (1710-11)*, ed. Agha Ahmad Ali, Bib. Ind., Calcutta, 1870-3, tr. J. Sarkar, Calcutta, 1947.
Saraswati, K., "Birds in Mughal Art", *MARG* (2), 1948.
Sarkar, B.K., *Inland Transport and Communication in Medieval India*, Calcutta, 1925.
Sarma, S.R., "Scientific Instruments, Evidence from Mughal Painting" in A.J. Qaisar and S.P. Verma (eds.), *Art and Culture, Painting and Perspective*, New Delhi, 2002.
Sarre, F. and F.R. Martin, *Die Ausstellung Von Meisterwerken Muhammedanischer Kunst in Munchen*, 1910, Munich, 1912.
Schroeder, Eric, "Paintings from the Hamza romance", *BFAM*, 9, 1941.
——, "The troubled image, an essay upon Mogul painting", *Art and Thought (A Commemorative Volume published in Honour of Ananda K. Coomaraswamy)*, K. Bhartha Iyer (ed.), London, 1947.
Schulberg, L., *Das Fruhe Indien*, Netherland, 1969.
Schulz, P.W., *Die Persisch—Islamische Miniaturmalerei*, Leipzig, 1914.
Scerrato, Umberto, "Mir Sayyid Ali", *EWA*, 10, 1968.
Sen, B., "The precursors of the Mughal school of painting", *S.P. Shah Commemoration Volume*, 1940.
Sen, G., "Mighty miniature of Akbar", *Orientations*, Hong Kong, June 1976.
——, "An unpublished study of a *sadhu* by Basawan and its relation to other drawings", *LALIT*, 20, New Delhi, 1982.
Seyller, John, "Model and copy: The illustration of three *Razmnama* manuscripts", *AAA*, 38, 1935.
——, "The School of Oriental and African Studies, *Anvar-i Suhayli*: The illustrations of a De Luxe Mughal Manuscript", *AAA*, Vol. XXXVIII, 1985.
——, "Recycled Images Overpainting in Early Mughal Art" in Canby Sheila (ed.), *Humayun's Garden Party, Princes of the House of Timur and Early Mughal Painting*, Bombay, 1994.
Shah Nawaz Khan, *Ma'asir ul Umara'* (1742-80), Abdu'r Rahim and Ashraf Ali (ed.), Bib. Ind., Calcutta, 1888-91; tr. H. Beveridge, Bib. Ind., Calcutta, 1911.
Shanti Swarup, *The Arts and Crafts of India and Pakistan*, Bombay, 1957.
——, *500 Years of Arts and Crafts in India and Pakistan*, Bombay, 1968.
——, *Flora and Fauna in Mughal Art*, Bombay, 1983.
——, *Indian Miniature Painting (Exhibition catalogue)*, Tokyo, 1973.
Simsar, A. Muhammed (tr. and ed.), *The Cleveland Museum of Art's Tuti-Nama, Tales of a Parrot*, Austria, 1978.
Simsar, A. and A.W. Brown, "Late Mughal illustrations to the *Iqbalnamah-i Jahangiri*", *JAOS*, 58, 1938.
Singh, Chandramani, "European themes in early Mughal miniatures", *Chhavi*, Banaras, 1971.
Skelton, Robert, "Mughal artist Farrokh Beg", *AOS*, 2, 1957.
——, "*The Ni'matnama:* A landmark in Malwa painting", *MARG*, 12 (3), 1959.
——, *Indian Miniatures from the XVth to XIXth Centuries*, Venice, 1961.
——, "Two Mughal lion hunts", *Victoria and Albert Museum Yearbook*, 1, London, 1969.
——, "Mughal paintings from the Harivamsa manuscript", *Victoria and Albert Museum Yearbook*, 2, London, 1970.
——, "A decorative motif in Mughal art" in Pratapaditya Pal (ed.), *Aspects of Indian Art*, Leiden, 1972.
——, "Indian painting of the Mughal period" in B.W. Robinson (ed.), *Islamic Painting and the Arts of the Book (The Keir Collection)*, London, 1976.

——, "Facets of Indian painting" in Denys Sutton (ed.), *Treasures from the Collection of Frits Lugt at the Institut Neerlandais, Paris*, London, 1976.
——, "*The Iskandar Nama* of Nusrat Shah" in M. Goedhuis (ed.), *Indian Painting (Mughal and Rajput and a Sultanate Manuscript)*, Colnaghi, London, 1978.
——, "Paintings in the arts of the book", *The Indian Heritage (Court Life and Arts under Mughal Rule), Catalogue of the exhibition held at the Victoria and Albert Museum, 21 April-22 August 1982*, Festival of India, London, 1982.
——, *The Indian Heritage, Court Life and Arts under Mughal Rule*, London, 1982.
——, *L'Inde des Legendes et des realites, Miniatures Indiennes et Persanes*, Paris, n.d.
Skelton, Robert, Andrew Topsfield, Susan Stronge, and Crill Rosemary (eds.), *Facets of Indian Art: A Symposium held at the Victoria and Albert Museum*, New Delhi, 1987.
Smart, E.S., "Six folios from a dispersed manuscript of the Baburnama" in M. Goedhuis (ed.), *Indian Painting (Mughal and Rajput and a Sultanate Manuscript)*, Colnaghi, London, 1978.
——, "Four illustrated *Baburnama* manuscript", *Art and Archaeology Research Papers*, 3, London, 1973.
——, "Akbar, the illiterate genius", *Kaladarsana*, Joanna Williams (ed.), New Delhi, 1981.
——, "A recently discovered Mughal hunting picture by Payag", *AH*, December 1979.
——, "Yet another illustrated Akbari *Baburnama* manuscript" in R. Skelton, *et al.* (eds.), *Facets of Indian Art: A Symposium held at the Victoria and Albert Museum*, London.
Smart, E.S. and Walkar, Daniel S., *Pride of the Princes: Indian Art of the Mughal Era in the Cincinnati Art Museum*, Ohio.
Smith, Edmund W., *Mogul Architecture of Fathpur Sikri*, Allahabad, 1984.
Smith, V.A., *A History of Fine Art in India and Ceylon*, Oxford, 1911.
——, "Remarks on Mogul (Indo-Persian) paintings and drawings (The Festival of Empire)", *JIA*, 15, 1913.
——, *Akbar, the Great Mogul (1542-1605)*, reprint, Delhi, 1962.
Smith, W., "Hindu ascetics in Mughal painting under Akbar", *OA*, New Series, 27, no. 1, London, 1981.
Soustiel, J., *Miniatures Orientales de l'Inde*, Paris, 1974.
——, *Miniatures Orientales de l'Inde: Les Ecoles et Leurs Styles*, Paris, 1973.
Srivastava, A.L., "Akbar's contribution to the theory of Kingship", *Uma Bharti*, Agra, Vol. II, No. 1, 1862.
——, *Medieval Indian Culture*, Jaipur, 1964.
Shrivastava, Ashok Kumar, *Mughal Painting, an Interplay of Indigenous and Foreign Traditions*, New Delhi, 2000.
Srivastava, R.P., *Punjab Painting*, Delhi, 1983.
Staude, W., "Abdus-Samad, der Akbar-Maler und des Millionen-zimmer in Schonbrunn", *Belvedere*, 10 (5), 1931.
——, "Contribution a l'etude de Basawan", *RAA*, 8 (1), 1934.
——, *Moghul Maler der Akbar Zeit*, Wien, 1935.
——, "Les artistes de la cour d'Akbar et les illustrations du Dastan-i Amir Hamzah", *ASA*, 1-2, 1955.
——, "Basawan", *EWA*, 2, 1960.
——, "Le Paysage dans l'Akbar-Namah", *RAA*, 5, 1928-9.
——, "Muskine", *RAA*, 5, 1929.
——, "Daswant", *EWA*, 4, 1960.
Stchoukine, I., *La Peinture Indienne a l'Epoque des Grands Moghols*, Paris, 1929.
——, *Les Miniatures Indiennes de l'Epoque des Grands Moghols du Musee du Louvre*, Paris, 1929.
——, "Quelques images de Jahangir dans in Divan de Hafiz", *Gazette des Beaux-Arts*, 6, Paris, 1931.
——, "Portraits Moghols Parts I-IV", *RAA*, VI (1929-30), VII (1931-2) and VIII (1935).
——, "Un Bustan de Sa'di illustre par des artistes Moghols", *RAA*, 11, 1937.
——, "Les peintures de *Shah-namah*", *ASA*, 5, 1958.
Strauss, W.L., *The Complete Engravings, Etchings and Drypoints of Albrecht Durer*, New York, 1972.
Strong, Roy, *The Victoria and Albert Museum: The Making of the Collection*, London, n.d.
Stronge, Susan, *Painting for the Mughal Emperor, the Art of the Book 1560-1660*, Delhi, 2002.
Strzygowski, J., H. Gluck, S. Kramrisch and E. Wellesz, *Asiatische Miniaturenmalerei*, Klagenfurt, 1933.
Suleiman, H., *Miniatures of the Babur-nama*, Tashkent, 1970.

Sykes, P.M., *History of Persia*, London, 1915.

Tavernor-Perry, T., "The Nimbus in Eastern Art", *BUM*, Vol. XII, No. LV, 1907.

Tchitcherov, Alexander I., *India, Changing Economic Structure in the Sixteenth-Eighteenth Centuries, Outline History of Crafts and Trade*, New Delhi, 1998.

Thapar, Romila, *Asoka and the Decline of the Mauryas*, New Delhi, 1961.

Thevenot, M. de, *Indian Travels of Thevenot and Careri*, ed. S. Sen, New Delhi, 1949.

The Voyage of Nicholas Downton to the East Indies, 1614-15, London, 1939.

Titley, Norah M., "An Illustrated Persian Glossary of the 16th Century", *British Museum Quarterly*, Vol. XXXIX, 1964-65.

——, *Miniatures from Persian Manuscripts (A catalogue and subject index of paintings from Persia, India and Turkey in the British Library and the British Museum)*, British Museum, London, 1977.

——, *Sports and Pastimes (Scenes from Turkish, Persian and Mughal Paintings)*, British Library, London, 1979.

——, *Plants and Gardens in Persian, Mughal and Turkish Art*, British Library, London, 1979.

——, *Persian Miniature Painting and its Influence on the Art of Turkey and India (The British Library Collection)*, London, 1984.

——, "Miniature paintings illustrating the works of Amir Khusrau: 15th, 16th, 17th centuries", *MARG*, XXVIII, no. 3, 1975.

Topsfield, Andrew, "Painting and the arts of the book" in *The Indian Heritage (Court Life and Arts under Mughal Rule), Catalogue of the Exhibition held at the Victoria and Albert Museum, 21 April-22 August 1982*, Festival of India, London, 1982.

——, (2) *An Introduction to Indian Court Painting*, London, 1984.

Trinkaus, Charles and Naomi Miller, "Humanism", *Encyclopaedia of World Art*, Mc-Graw Hill Company Inc., London, 1963.

Troll, Christian W. (ed.), *Islam in India, Studies and Commentaries*, New Delhi, 1982.

Tyulayev, S.I., *Indian Art in Soviet Collections*, Moscow, 1956.

——, "Miniatures from a 16th century manuscript Baburnama", *MARG*, 11 (3), 1958.

——, *Miniatures of Babur Nama*, Moscow, 1960.

Valle, Pietro della (1623), *The Travels of Pietro delle Valle in India*, ed. Gray Edward, and tr. G. Havers, London, 1892.

Vania, Eugenia, *Urban Crafts and Craftsmen in Medieval India (13th-18th Centuries)*, New Delhi, 2004.

Varma, D.N., "A painting by the Mughal artist Farrukh Chela", *ISC*, 58 (2), Hyderabad, 1984.

Vaughan, Philippa, "Mythical Animal in Mughal Art: Images Symbols and Allusions" in S.P. Verma (ed.), *Flora and Fauna in Mughal Art*, Mumbai, 1999.

Verma, S.P., "Wine-pots at the Mughal Court in the Sixteenth Century", *Medieval India—a miscelleny*, Vol. III, New Delhi, 1973.

——, "*Chela* painters of the Mughal Court", *PIHC*, Aligarh, 1975.

——, "Miniatures of the *Tarikh-i Khandan-i Timuria*", *ROOPA*, 43 (1-2), 1976.

——, "Who were '*chela*' painters", *QRHS*, 16 (3), 1976-7.

——, "Farrukh the *chela* painter of Akbar's court", *QRHS*, 16 (4), 1977-8.

——, "*Anwar-i Suhaili*—an illustrated manuscript of Akbar's Court in the collection of Bharat Kala Bhavan, Varanasi", *ROOPA*, Vol. XLIV, Nos. 1-2, 1977.

——, "Introduction of self-portrait painting in India", *PIHC*, Bhubaneswar, 1977.

——, "Farrukh Beg—the Mughal court painter", *PIHC*, Hyderabad, 1978.

——, *Art and Material Culture in the Paintings of Akbar's Court*, New Delhi, 1978.

——, "An illustrated manuscript of the *Diwan-i-Hafiz* of Akbar's court in the collection of Wali Ahad Rampur", *ROOPA*, 50 (1-2), 1978-9.

——, "Margin-painting in medieval Indian art", *PIHC*, Waltair, 1979.

——, "Portraits of the calligraphers depicted in the Mughal miniatures—a historical study", *ISC*, 54 (3), 1980.

——, "Illustrated *Akbarnama* of sixteenth century Mughal school", *ROOPA*, 51 (1-2), 1980.

——, "Self-portrait painting in India" (based on the illustrated lecture delivered at the Victoria Memorial Hall, Calcutta, 20 November 1979), *BVM*, 13, 1979.

——, "Fire-Arms in Sixteenth Century India (A study based on Mughal Paintings of Akbar's period", *Islamic Culture*, Vol. 57, No. 1, 1983.

——, "Sixteenth century Mughal miniatures at Royal Library, Windsor and India Office Library—a survey of hitherto unnoticed miniatures", *PIHC*, Bodh-Gaya, 1981; *ROOPA*, 57 (1-2), 1985.

——, "Painters under Khan-i Khanan", *QRHS*, 20 (1), 1980-1.

——, "Mansur, the master-painter of Jahangir's epoch", *ROOPA*, 53 (1-2), 1982.

——, "Elements of historicity in the portraits of the Mughal school", *IHR* 9 (1-2), 1982-3.

——, "Artists' signatures in the Miniatures of the Mughal School", *IHR*, Vol.X, Nos. 1&2, 1983-84.

——, "Mughal margin-painting (a study based on the miniatures at Victoria Memorial)", *Victoria Memorial Hall* (Diamond Jubilee Souvenir Volume, 1921-1981), Calcutta, 1984.

——, "Self-portraits by Mughal court painters", *ROOPA*, 56 (1-2), 1984.

——, "Technology in Mughal India—evidence of Mughal painting" in Aniruddha Roy and S.K. Bagchi (eds.), *Technology in Ancient and Medieval India*, Delhi, 1986.

——, "Seventeenth century illustrated manuscript: the *Padshahnama*", *ROOPA*, 58 (1-2), 1986.

——, "Khwaja Abdu-s Samad – Court Painter of Sixteenth Century", *ROOPA*, Vol. LIX, Nos. 1&2, 1987.

——, "Aspects of paintings in the British Museum Manuscript of the *Akbarnama*", *LALIT*, No.27, 1993.

——, "Origins of the Mughal School of Painting" in A.J. Qaisar and S.P. Verma (eds.), *Art and Culture, Felicitation Volume in Honour of Professor S. Nurul Hasan*, Jaipur, 1993.

——, *Mughal Painters and Their Work: A Bibliographical Survey and Comprehensive Catalogue*, New Delhi, 1994.

——, *India at Work in Sculpture and Painting*, Aligarh, 1994.

——, "Painting under Akbar as Narrative Art" in Irfan Habib (ed.), *Akbar and His India*, New Delhi, 1997.

——, "Lal, the Forgotten Master" in Asok K. Das (ed.), *Mughal Masters: Further Studies*, Mumbai, 1998.

——, "Akbar's School of Painting: Mughal Vision and Approach" in Iqtidar Alam Khan (ed.), *Akbar and His Age*, New Delhi, 1999.

——, (ed.), *Flora and Fauna in Mughal Art*, Mumbai, 1999.

——, "The Tulip [ca.1621]: A Study by Mansur", *Huntia*, Pittsburgh, Vol. 9 (1), 1993; see also *Huntia*, 10 (2), 1999. See also *MARG*, Vol. XLVI, No. 4, pp. 81-4.

——, *Mughal Painter of Flora and Fauna, Ustad Mansur*, New Delhi, 1999.

——, "Illustrations of Persian Classics in Persian and Imperial Mughal Painting" in Muzaffar Alam, Francoise Nalini Delvoye, and Marc Gaborieau (eds.), *The Making of Indo-Persian Culture, Indian and French Studies*, New Delhi, 2000.

——, "Portraits of Ordinary Men from the Sixteenth Century Mughal School", *ROOPA*, Vol. Nos. XLVII-LXXI, 2001.

——, "Mughal Painting, Patrons and Painters", *PIHC*, Kolkata, 2001.

——, "The *Miftah-ul Fuzala*, a Study of an Illustrated Lexion", jointly with Ahsan Jan Qaisar in Ahsan Jan Qaisar and S.P. Verma (eds.), *Art and Culture: Painting and Perspective*, Delhi, 2002.

——, "Symbols and Motifs in Mughal School of Art" in Ahsan Jan Qaisar and S.P. Verma (eds.), *Art and Culture: Painting and Perspective*, Delhi, 2002.

——, "Similar Themes, Different Treatment" in Ahsan Jan Qaisar and S.P. Verma (eds.), *Art and Culture: Painting and Perspective*, Delhi, 2002.

——, "Ordinary Life in Mughal India" in Ahsan Jan Qaisar and S.P. Verma (eds.), *Art and Culture: Painting and Perspective*, Delhi, 2002.

——, "Persian and Mughal Painting: The Fundamental Relationship" in Irfan Habib (ed.), *A Shared Heritage, the Growth of Civilization in India and Iran*, New Delhi, 2002.

——, "Humanism in Mughal Painting", *PIHC* (Amritsar, 2002), Kolkata, 2003.

——, *Painting the Mughal Experience*, New Delhi, 2005.

Visser, H.F.E., "Tentoonstelling der kunst van India te Londen", *Phoenix*, 3 (1), February 1948.

Wade, Bonnie C., *An Ethnomusicological Imaging Study of Music, Art, and Sound Culture in Mughal*, London, 1998.

Warner, G., *Descriptive Catalogue of Illuminated Manuscripts in the Library of C.W. Dyson Perrins*, 2 (134), Oxford, 1920 (includes note on *Khamsa* of Nizami, Or. 12208).

Welch, S.C., "Miniatures from a manuscript of the *Diwan-i Hafiz*", *MARG*, 11 (3), 1958.

——, "Early Mughal miniature paintings from two private collections shown at the Fogg Art Museum", *AOS*, 3, 1959.
——, "The emperor Akbar's *Khamsa* of Nizami", *JWAG*, 1959.
——, "The paintings of Basawan", *LALIT*, 10, 1963.
——, "Mughal and Deccani miniature paintings from a private collection", *AOS*, 5, 1963.
——, *The Art of Mughal India: Painting and Precious Objects (Catalogue of an exhibition shown in the galleries of Asia House, New York during the winter of 1964)*, New York, 1963.
——, *A Flower from Every Meadow, Indian Painting From American Collections (Catalogue of the exhibition shown in the galleries of Asia House, New York, 1973)*, New York, 1973.
——, *Indian Drawings and Painted Sketches (16th Through 19th Centuries)*, New York, 1976.
——, *Imperial Mughal Painting*, London, 1978.
——, *India, Art and Culture (1300-1900), Catalogue of the exhibition "India" held at The Metropolitan Museum of Art from September 14, 1985 to January 5, 1986)*, New York, 1985.
Welch, S.C. and M.C. Beach, *Gods, Thrones and Peacocks (Catalogue of an exhibition held in Asia House Gallery, New York, from 23rd September to 12th December, 1965; Baltimore Museum of Art, from 18th January to 27th February and Munson-Williams-Proctor Institute, Utica, New York, from 3rd April to 15th May, 1966)*, New York, 1965.
Welch, S.C. and A. Schimmel, *Anvari's Divan: A Pocket Book of Akbar*, New York, 1983.
Welch, S.C., A. Schimmel, Swietochowski and W.M. Thackston, *The Emperors' Album, Images of Mughal India*, New York, 1987.
Wellesz, Emmy, "An *Akbar-Namah* manuscript", *BUM*, 80, 1942.
——, "Mughal paintings at Burlington House", *BUM*, 90 (539), 1948.
——, *Akbar's Religious Thought Reflected in Mughal Painting*, Oxford, 1952.
Werner, Alfred, *Indian Miniatures*, New York, 1950.
Wilkinson, J.V.S., "The British Indian Union exhibition of Indian paintings", *RUPAM*, 40, 1929.
——, *The Lights of Canopus: Anwar-i Suhaili*, London, 1929.
——, "A dated illustrated manuscript of Akbar's reign", *JISOA*, 2 (2), 1934.
——, "An Indian manuscript of the Golestan of the Shah Jahan period", *AOS*, 2, 1957.
——, "Indian painting", *Indian Art Essay*, 1947.
——, *Mughal Painting*, London, 1948.
——, "Indian painting" in Richard Winstedt (ed.), *Indian Art*, London, 1966.
——, "A note on an illustrated manuscript of *Jog-Bashisht*", *BSOS*, 12, 1968.
Williams, L.F. Rushrook, *An Empire Builder of the Sixteenth Century*, Allahabad, 1978.
——, (ed.), *The Great Men of India*, Ceylon, n.d.
Wilson, Ralph Pinder, "Mughal India", *Arts of The Islamic World*, 3 (2), London, 1985.
Winstedt, R. (ed.), *Indian Art*, London, 1947.
Wolf, R.E., *Islam and Muslim Art* (tr. from French), London, 1980.
Yasin, Mohammad, *A Social History of Islamic India, 1605-1748*, Lucknow, 1958.
Zaman, F.U., "Nafa'isal Ma'asir", *INI*, 15 (4), 1962.
Zimmer, Heinrich, *The Art of Indian Asia: Its Mythology and Transformations*, New York, 1955.

Index